THE ART OF RETREATING

THE ART OF RETREATING

A Field Guide to Calm in a Time of Chaos

JACQUELINE HEIL

ISBN 9780578879987

Also available as an ebook: 9780578898254

DEDICATION

This book is dedicated to my father Peter who taught me through his example the value and transformative power of love, compassion, forgiveness, grace, awe and wonder, and how to find peace within myself despite my circumstances.

—Birds and Trees

To *my* caregiver and my rock, my husband Mark, who keeps me moored when the waters are choppy.

—I love you beyond words

This book is also dedicated to Ashley and Lillian, my father's selfless caregivers, who have shepherded my father and our family through adversity, challenges, and obstacles, many times shouldering the weight and carrying our burdens on this journey. They and others are guides who light the way out of darkness.

—You are part of my rooted heart community

To each and every caregiver in the world and all of the frontline essential workers.

—No other words, thank you.

Your Intentions Need Attention.

Your Journey Awaits...

CONTENTS

INTRODUCTION

As our daily routines and lifestyles are upended, it is not surprising to feel unmoored. Now more than ever, it is increasingly important to regard yourself as the sacred being that you are. Finding calm, peace, and restorative rest have become necessary life skills, not luxuries for a privileged few. They are essential to our overall well-being.

At the start of the year 2020, I personally was in transition from one season of my life to the next. I was completing my work for a global meditation institute as an operations director and fanning the flames of what I believed would be the next step of my journey, that is, creating opportunities for myself and others to find calm in the chaos, drawing from my own life experiences and lessons.

The purpose of this new business idea is to inspire joy, offer support, provide nourishment, and a path to peace in the wake of the challenges that each of us face in times of transitions. The goal is to focus on the essentials that we as caregivers need in order for our own well-being.

Little did I know when I chartered this course, of the impending global events that would unfold in the form of a pandemic. In the wake of uncertainty, fear, and trauma precipitated by the uncontrollable spread of a worldwide virus, we all had no choice but to stop and acknowledge Nature's force. In my case, the universe stepped up and delivered my marching orders on a grander scale than I could ever imagine. Thank you, universe.

The pandemic has catapulted our levels of stress and anxiety to an astronomical level and left us in a collective state of uncertainty. Like you, I halted all plans and attended to the priorities of ensuring the safety of my family, including my elderly father with dementia; transitioning my remaining assignments with the Institute; accommodating my husband's new reality of working from home; and beginning to discern how this pandemic would impact life as we know it, as well as our future.

With stay at home orders, travel restrictions, and no clear understanding about the long-term effects of the pandemic, it was clear that I could not start the enterprise I had envisioned. With my plans on hold, I tried to keep busy and remained open to what was to come. On a restless afternoon, I started to formulate some of the ideas for my business. When one is not attached too closely to form, something else can emerge. Maybe something better.

I quickly realized that the knowledge and resources I possess to start a physical business could be organized and shared in the form of a book. As I started writing, the words came pouring out, as if they had been there all along. Writing provided the structure I yearned for in this turbulent time. It became my mission and my purpose each and every day. **The Art of Retreating** provides the roadmap to reach the oasis where we can rest and fill ourselves up from the wellspring of life. It is a simple, straightforward guide to point out what you may be missing when you are *out in the field* caring for loved ones, or when your own reserves are depleted.

There are still waters within you that you can tap if you know how to find the well. Through the seven primary practices outlined in the following chapters, you will find the means to develop deep contentment and a sense of certainty, regardless of what is going on around you. Inner peace equates to outer calm and when you are calm, you shine brightly for yourself and those around you. We need your light.

The Art of Retreating helps you to recognize a chaotic brain and other signs of burnout, anxiety, and overwhelm, so that you can take action to lessen the impact of troubling experiences on your being. Practices presented in the field guide and notes assist you in refreshing your mind, body and spirit so that you can bring your best self to the world. It provides tips for centering yourself even in the midst of extreme fear, trauma, chaos and transitions. By focusing on what is really important to you and what you care about, you will be more aligned with your true values and the essence of your authentic self, rather than those of others.

In its simplest form, the field guide presents techniques and suggestions for quality rest, renewal, and ways to gently tend to ourselves. I refer to this as *embodied awakening* or just being. If we don't have the time to rest, refuel and nurture our aspirations, then how are we able to dream and see the possibility for our futures?

I am a cheerleader, coach, and helpful spirit greatly invested in your well-being. As I am not trained in the fields of medicine, mental health or crisis management, please note that this book is not a substitute for professional care, counseling and medical help for any issues you may be enduring personally, or for that of a loved one. Serious medical or mental health issues, as well as crisis management, should be addressed with the guidance of qualified professionals. I have included resources for crisis management and grief counseling in the field notes of Chapter 12, for anyone who is not sure where to begin.

We are building a community of souls who unapologetically give themselves permission to put self-care at the top of their list of priorities. This is a movement which not only benefits our own interests, but those of everyone in our orbit. The positive effects ripple out and touch us all! I wish you well on this journey. Life will continue to ebb and flow for each of us. There will be uncertainty and events outside of our control. When the time comes to find refuge and restoration, may this book serve as a reliable guide to return to again and again.

Now dear one, are you ready to run away with me and find the oasis that will soothe your weary body, mind and spirit?

1

I DID NOT SIGN UP FOR THIS

"Nothing flutters into a cluttered life. The frantic and exhausted mind does not possess the energy to inspire a love-filled path."
—TAMA J. KIEVES

Yesterday I was under siege. My sympathetic nervous system was triggered by a traumatic event which sent me into a tailspin. Even though I am a seasoned veteran in dealing with crisis management and chaos, I found myself so caught off guard, I was incapable of implementing one of the tried and true tactics that I typically utilize to manage stress.

The day started with a peaceful walk along the waterfront with my husband and our dog, Harley. It had been one of the few ways we found solace during the stay at home orders related to the worldwide pandemic. We live in the city, in San Diego, and gravitate to the water for our walks to enjoy a wide open panorama of sea and sky. It offers both of us peace and refuge.

Rounding our building on the way home, I noticed a woman laying on her back on a yoga mat with her attention completely absorbed in her phone. I noticed two dogs lying on the mat as well, eyes locked on us while guarding their owner. As we walked by, the dogs launched off of the mat tethered to one another, charging directly towards us. They began attacking my dog. The woman had no control of the leash. One of the dogs aggressively bit Harley on the hind quarters while the other one barked viciously at my husband.

In response and utter fear, I began to kick the attacking dog. I swept Harley up in my arms to get him out of harm's way, but the leash of the other dog was wrapped tightly around my leg in a double bind with the dog's head close to my body. It was a frightening chaotic scene. By this time, the woman realized what was happening, sprang to her feet and began yelling at us as we tried to deal with the situation. I was shocked at her violent and aggressive response and her attempt to physically threaten us. She was badgering my husband with profanity, challenging him to a physical fight. I was praying that he would not take the bait, which would only make matters worse.

The adrenaline was pulsing through my body, while my brain was trying to process how to escape these threats coming at us all at once. I didn't know which was the greater danger, the dogs or their owner? Within a few feet of me were an aggressive woman with the physique of a bodybuilder, her two dogs, with mouths full of sharp teeth, and my unnerved husband who was trying to protect me and our dog. It was difficult to process and prioritize which threat was most real and how to diffuse the situation. Thinking quickly, I was able to convince the woman to remove the leash from my leg and we immediately fled the scene. Thankfully, things did not escalate because we chose not to engage with her. We returned home with cortisol pulsing through our bodies, upset, but gratefully, more or less unharmed.

Unfortunately this was the second time my dog had been attacked in the past month and both incidents were quite traumatic. In the ensuing hours, I could not regain my calm. I felt violated, fearful and angry. What's worse is that it revived the trauma from the prior experience which I had still not fully processed. During that incident, an unleashed dog of a homeless man viciously attacked my dog leaving him with puncture wounds in his back. Both my husband and I threw ourselves between the two dogs to break it up. These are things that you shouldn't do, but when a situation occurs so quickly, you react instinctively.

After venting to my husband, who was also reeling from the experience, I tried deep breathing techniques. That didn't work. I went out on our patio and practiced mindfulness and meditation, to no avail. The incident played on a loop in my head, preventing me from relaxing. I continued to relive the experience and feel the heightened adrenaline from both attacks. This was not helping. Clearly, everything I knew and regularly practiced about disarming these emotions was not working.

Eventually I gave up and headed to bed at one o'clock that afternoon. It was the only way I knew how to disconnect completely from what had occurred. At that point, I was desperately trying to forget the experience all together. I fell into a deep sleep. That power nap of ninety minutes or so severed the playback loop in my mind and provided a retreat from the trauma I had experienced. My body relaxed for a little while and I woke up feeling much better, as if it was a new day. That nap was my oasis when nothing else seemed to help. It was an act of self-love that nurtured and supported me in a time of need.

Typically, I have a go-go-go personality and make the most of every waking moment. Until the past few years, napping has always seemed like a waste of valuable time. Now it is an essential component of retreating from the many challenges that have become part of my life. Even a five minute power nap has the ability to transform a mood, stop a looping negative thought, or calm the aftermath of a stressful experience. Napping is just one of the many tools that I reach for when I need to retreat from something, someone, or even myself! Like many other rituals and tactics to be discussed in the following pages, napping simply works. By stepping away and recalibrating, we shift our energy to better serve ourselves and the world.

Today, we are living with extreme amounts of daily stress, more than most of us have experienced in our lifetime. Each day we are barraged by a multitude of responsibilities and unexpected events, such as bad news, a sick family member, unexpected financial obligations, health issues, identity theft, invasion of privacy or some other calamity that completely derails us. We are experiencing uncertainty on a global level, as well as collective economic and socio-economic strife that we have never seen before. It's difficult to reassure those who depend on us when we ourselves are unsure. The secret to maintaining a sense of calm and centeredness is to put your own needs first. To do this is not a selfish act as long as it does not cause harm. In fact, self-love and self-care create a better version of each of us so that we can be more present and engaged in the lives of others.

On the positive side (and in the pre-pandemic world), there are lots of wonderful things that also fill our cups to the brim, like our family celebrations and milestones, recitals, Little League games, seeing friends, or volunteering for a wonderful organization, just to name a few. But ALL of these things require our time, attention, and prioritization. Most of us are in perpetual overload.

Life is messy and it doesn't always unfold as we would like. There are surprises along the way which require us to recalculate our route and change our plans. There isn't one among us that is exempt from this fact of life. If you are human, misfortune or challenges will occur at some point in your life. While it may appear that some people coast through life, eventually they too will have adversity or obstacles to face. It's just part of our human experience. If we come to accept that the difficulties and uninvited events are part of the growth and development of our souls, it is possible to reframe these experiences with resilience, grace and fortitude.

In order to navigate the highs and lows, the unforeseen circumstances, and the uncertainty of life, it's essential to draw from our own internal resources, fortifying those key traits I just mentioned, resilience, grace and fortitude. That, my friend, requires self-care. Not self-indulgence, not selfishness, but self-care which invokes self-love and an understanding of our own unique needs. Each of us has our own particular needs. We are unique individuals responding to life's challenges in our own way with the coping skills we have derived through our upbringing and experiences. And what's more, our needs will continue to change like the seasons. Growth is dynamic, ever-evolving. If we are not growing, we are dying.

I want to share another personal story which illustrates the need for self care. We are all familiar with the adage, *put your own oxygen mask on first before helping others.* To state it another way, you can't help someone else, if you yourself, are flailing. A few years ago, I learned first hand what this means.

After living in the same home for thirty-five years, it was time for my father to move. My parents had amassed a lifetime of memories and "stuff" within the walls of a 4,500 sq. ft. home in Memphis, Tennessee. It fell to me to orchestrate this monumental transition. I had been traveling back and forth across the country for several years after my mom passed in 2010, to organize and downsize family possessions. My sister and I had to go through every square inch of that house and help my father decide what he would take to a 1,200 sq. ft. condominium in San Diego. The move was prompted by a dementia diagnosis and a recommendation that he live closer to family. Within that year, I made several cross-country trips to orchestrate all of the logistics including an estate sale and the sale of his home. Simultaneously, I had also started a brand new job as the Director of Strategic Operations for a global meditation institution. In addition, I had not fully recovered from a previous very demanding and stressful job. During this time, I felt a bit like a firefighter putting out one brushfire after another.

The days leading up to the actual move were frenzied and long as I juggled logistics, work, family, and household commitments. Moves, in general, are some of the most stressful transitions we face. There was so much work to be done at the house right up to the last moments, as well as many farewell parties and goodbyes within his community. I wanted to ensure a beautiful and smooth transition for my father to lessen the difficulty of this giant change. As an empath, I felt depleted and emotional as I shouldered the pain and sadness my father was feeling in closing out this central chapter of his life.

On moving day, shortly after the movers arrived, a rusty metal fertilizer spreader weighing seventy pounds fell off of the garage wall and hit me on my head, slicing the left side of my skull above my ear. I didn't see it coming but I certainly felt the impact! Thank goodness my brother and some movers were close by, heard me shriek and were able to lift it off of me.

Rather than orchestrating the move as planned, I spent most of that day in the E.R. undergoing tests and having my head stitched up. I was very lucky that my head injury was not worse than it was. My brother drove me to the emergency room, leaving my cognitively declining father alone to direct the movers as to what to put on the moving truck. Many of the items that we planned to leave behind and sell ended up on the moving truck and eventually in San Diego because neither my brother nor I were there to direct the move. Instead, I had a significant concussion with a three month recovery ahead of me.

Sometimes, what we think is our mission, goes sideways. We find ourselves saying, "I didn't sign up for this!" Or we're overwhelmed by dealing with too many things at one time.

The lesson here is had I taken care of myself during this very physically and mentally demanding time (as in, put my own oxygen mask on first), I probably would not have been so exhausted and may have averted an extremely debilitating accident. Fortunately, I recovered fully and now realize the value of this experience.

What we really need is to develop coping skills and resiliency to get through life's unforeseen and unplanned events. If we have a field guide of options, we'll have resources to support us through these inevitable battles. *Retreating* is a tactical, defensive, military operation, which allows troops to withdraw to occupy ground that is more easily defended. When we retreat, we are creating more ideal conditions to defend our own sanity and wellbeing.

Each of us should develop a supportive pathway from fight or flight to a place of presence and calm.

Think of this book as your navigational guide for reorienting yourself with self-compassion and care, finding your inner refuge in the process.

My younger self did not understand this and so for a long time I found myself ping ponging through challenging experiences in a reactive, exhaustive manner. Typically this resulted in feeling depleted, sick, depressed and burnt out. I would have to hit bottom and then pull myself up again and again. It didn't occur to me to ask, "What am I doing to take care of myself?" I just forged onto the next battle, with no game plan. I was taking care of everything and everyone, and leaving myself undone. In hindsight, through a long journey of trial and error, I have found a better way which I am inspired to share with you.

I wonder, do you regularly ask, "What am I doing to take care of myself?"

Well for starters, how do you start your day? Do your plans get sidetracked easily? How is your mood? Are you getting enough sleep? Are you getting out and exercising? A good indicator of self-care is how you are responding or reacting to the ones around you, namely your kids, your partner, your pet, your co-worker, your sister, your boss, your mother, your neighbor, and the guy driving the car in front of you.

There are clear symptoms and warning signs of depletion, brought on by unrelenting fight or flight experiences for most caregivers and those experiencing transition or crisis, including irritability, impatience, anxiety, lack of focus, short temper, pessimism, self-doubt, to name a few. Does this ring any bells? When we find ourselves out of alignment there are ways to re-center and restore our inner reserves.

Self-care requires compassion and reflection. It's essential to our wellbeing to prioritize our needs and give ourselves that time to recharge and decompress from the overload we are facing whether consciously or unconsciously. We must embody the mantra - *be still and know*. If we fail to do so, eventually the tank will run out of gas and we will be stranded. The key is to keep the tank filled and humming along as best we can. Just like the cars we drive, we all need tuneups. I have friends who believe this is self-indulgent nonsense, but I see the toll life takes on each of them; the chronic back ache; the weekly migraines; the constant fatigue. These external symptoms are the manifestation of built-up emotional stress that is not being relieved.

This is particularly imperative for those of us who are caregivers because we are constantly providing for others and depleting ourselves in the process. Caregivers are moms and dads; frontline nurses and doctors; paramedics; police and firemen; those caring for a sick, disabled or elderly family member; those supporting a loved one through grief or a crisis; or individuals in need within your community.

What we need to learn is the ***"Art of Retreating,"*** a practice that I have cultivated during difficult experiences over the past decade and beyond. The simple and practical techniques and rituals outlined here are intended to be a lifeline in the face of transitions, overload, chaos, and stress. They work equally well as proactive practices you can routinely do to avoid the burnout from physical and emotional stressors, in order to maintain balance. There are a multitude of resources you can draw upon, depending on the circumstances you are dealing with personally.

We must consciously be willing to retreat for a period of time from the demands of life, whether in the moment, for a day, a weekend, or longer. This book is a field guide to help you identify what you need, how to access it, and examples of self-nurturing that are tried and true. Each of these tools provides access to an inner oasis that assists us with refilling the *energetic well*. How do you know if it will work for you? Only through experimentation and practice. My goal is to introduce these resources to you, provide simple and easy ways to incorporate them in your life, and encourage you to create a sustainable routine as a foundation. You will then be able to draw upon them when you need them.

FIELD NOTES ON SELF-CARE

Whenever possible, give yourself permission to opt out of time commitments which are not aligned with your personal values and which do not serve you.

What can you eliminate? Well, start with anything that drains your energy. Here are just a few ideas...

- An unhealthy relationship (friend, family, co-worker)
- Clutter of any sort (physical, mental)
- Screen time (bad news, violence, oversaturation, inactivity)
- Judgment (about ourselves or anybody else)
- Shopping (do you need all that stuff? Is it life enhancing? Can you afford it? Is it meaningful and useful?)
- Something perhaps you did not sign up for. Maybe you begrudgingly said yes to something when your heart was telling you no.
- Social media (we all love it, but how much of it is beneficial? Screen time is a well documented addiction now).

Be intentional about your priorities and your pursuits in life. Freeing yourself up from thirty minutes of scrolling through your social media allows time to walk in nature and to recharge. Can you find some quiet time midday to catch your breath, or carve out fifteen minutes at the beginning of your day to try a little meditation? Can you reduce what is not benefiting you thereby making space for things that do?

I have a single litmus test for everything that comes into my life. I ask myself this question:

"Does this fill me up or deplete me?"

I can use this assessment for just about anything; relationships, work, activities, travel, and purchases. If I don't get a resounding yes, I will decline or pass on anything that I am unsure about. I simply walk away. This is how we use our own inner guidance system to steer clear of people, experiences and things that do not enhance our lives.

Each of us can carve out and cultivate some space in our lives, if we just take a little time to evaluate what we are presently doing in contrast to our priorities. Live your priorities with intention and conviction and be unapologetic about it. In doing so, the world will benefit greatly.

2

LESSONS OF A SAMURAI WARRIOR

"Mind Your Mind — When you manage to overcome your own mind, you overcome myriad concerns, rise above all things, and are free. When you are overcome by your own mind, you are burdened by myriad concerns, subordinate to things, unable to rise above. 'Mind your mind; guard it resolutely. Since it is the mind that confuses the mind, don't let your mind give in to your mind.'"

—SUZUKI SHOSAN, SAMURAI WARRIOR (1579-1655)

Let's discuss optimal performance. Our society is obsessed with optimizing performance whether it be in business or the physical conditioning of our bodies. There are performance enhancing supplements, technically designed shoes, clothes and equipment, self-improvement videos, seminars, webinars, online courses, master classes, podcasts and many other sources of inspirational guidance and how-to knowledge available to all. Maintaining a competitive edge has been so drilled into us through mass marketing, that most of us believe we must constantly be improving our game in order to measure up.

Frankly, there is a lot of unwarranted pressure fabricated by the industries that benefit from our need to perform, compete and *get ahead*. Our obsession for optimal performance fuels billion dollar industries including sportswear and sneaker companies, fitness centers, the food and beverage industry, health supplements and many motivational speakers and conferences held around the world. While all of these resources *are* inspirational and do enhance our performance in different ways, there are other ways to measure and account for our performance and stature. It's the difference between approaching our place in the world with a *collective* rather than a *competitive* mindset. That is to say, consider how our actions and experiences can benefit all who are in a relationship with us, rather than the *I win, you lose* mentality.

There is one simple secret to optimizing performance which accounts for the *collective* benefit, and it is a fundamental tenet of the age-old practice of the samurai warrior. It is the art of being *calm*. When one moves from a centered space of calmness, a broader field of observations emerge, as does the ability to respond more skillfully to anything one encounters. In **Aikido**, which is a form of peaceful martial arts, warriors train the body but also use the body to train the mind, and thereby calm the spirit. Aikido emanates from a place of centeredness, unity, harmony, and absolute peace. It is considered a spiritual martial art as it teaches us to view things on a higher level and look at them in totality.

As the warrior class of feudal Japan, the samurai have become mythical in their reputation for personal fortitude and toughness on the battlefield. The samurai warrior is exemplary of the great mindset and rigorous training necessary to be successful in war. *Bushido* is the code of honor and morals of the samurai warrior. It consists of eight guiding principles. The eighth of these guiding virtues is *self-control* and is essential to pursue and exemplify the other seven principles. While it is important to embody all of the principles, without self-control and the ability to be calm in the face of adversity, one cannot make strategic, calculated decisions and thoughtful responses to the unfolding events and threats in life. For a samurai warrior, this is the difference between life and death. That could apply to us, and those in our care, as well. Being calm allows us to take definitive action. We have a multitude of decisions to make from the moment we awake until we go to sleep. In the calm and focused mind, a clear blueprint of inspiration and solutions arise. In a scattered, tired and overworked mind, the decisions may be reactive, lacking judgment, or ultimately, life threatening. You can read more about *bushido* in a book entitled *Training the Samurai Mind: A Bushido Sourcebook* by Thomas Cleary.[1]

The samurai warrior philosophy is enduring and pragmatic, given its more than 500 year history. Suzuki Shōsan, a Japanese Zen priest who was born in 1579 into a samurai warrior family, is renowned for his advocacy of the disciplined mind, which he referred to as the *diamond hard wisdom mind*. He, like many other descendants of the samurai tradition, emphasizes the principle of *minding the mind* as a form of self-control. The challenge of minding the mind requires tremendous discipline. It can seem impossible at times. How are we to be calm and focused if our minds are racing all over the place? Further, if one is not well rested, the cognitive function of the mind declines significantly. Compound that with stress, crisis, or other negative factors and I guarantee that we will not be optimizing our performance and response on any level. Typically, a frazzled mind creates a downward spiral which then wreaks havoc on our emotional intelligence. I don't know about you, but when my emotions spiral out of control, it is much more difficult to re-center and get my feet on the ground. Recovery requires far more energy and effort.

1 *Training the Samurai Mind: A Bushido Sourcebook* by Thomas Cleary

With its origins in Buddhist principles, the *monkey mind* is a term that refers to a very unsettled mind which is restless and racing around. If we are experiencing monkey mind, we are highly distracted and will find it challenging to maintain focus or to make clear decisions. Many people find themselves victims of the monkey mind in the middle of the night, a time when their minds and bodies should be in a restorative, receptive state. *Being calm* and *minding the mind* require self-control, discipline, and practice. Practitioners of meditation and mindfulness know this very well.

The noble samurai warriors have been writing about calming the mind for centuries. In yet another fascinating book about the samurai warrior, *The Book of Five Rings* by Miyamoto Masashi[2], one of the greatest samurai warriors of history writes:

> *Both in fighting and in everyday life you should be determined though calm. Meet the situation without tenseness yet not recklessly, your spirit settled yet unbiased.*

This is an insightful guide to building resiliency. Having a settled spirit allows for perspective and to see the broader picture. Anything that we approach with resistance is more difficult to deal with energetically.

2 *The Book of Five Rings* by Miyamoto Masashi

You can find many other great examples of calmness woven through the historic tapestry of the noble samurai warriors. They seem to share the notion that this guiding principle is the key to survival. For them, it was truly about life and death. They referred to the need for vitality, courage, and "death energy," the readiness to confront death at any moment. It stems from the idea that if you face the very real fact that you are going to die, and prepare in every way for that outcome, then fear subsides and there is truly nothing to be afraid of. Research has shown that there are powerful techniques for promoting calm within the mind. One way is to imagine the absolute worst thing that can happen. If you follow the logical downward progression of consequences, you may realize that things are really not as bad as they seem. The contemplation of "what's the worst thing that can happen?" can help you to explore all options and dispel some of the fear.

This is how the samurai trained. Preparation of any sort reduces fear. If you prepare for a presentation and rehearse it over and over, it reduces the fear of public speaking and puts you more at ease. You may still experience some jitters but deep down the repetition and reinforcement provide a foundation of confidence. Likewise, the samurai warriors practiced and practiced for battle. They were well prepared for many different scenarios of attack and in a much better position of strength because of their discipline of hard work.

In fact, samurais trained relentlessly until their death. They earned the badge of calmness. Fear can be very motivating. The most powerful way to COMBAT stress or anxiety is to just remain calm. It provides a reassuring sense of control.

By now you may be wondering what all of this samurai warrior training has to do with a field guide for retreating and self-care. If there has ever been a time in history when we are collectively experiencing a deficiency of calm, it is now. Our society is in a constant state of anti-calming activities powered by information overload, caffeinated drinks, smart devices, and of course some of my favorites: life-altering bad news pumped out at us 24/7 from a variety of "news" sources and divergent politics that are increasingly polarizing. Not surprisingly, drug use, addiction and suicide rates are on the rise. In 2020, the divorce rate went up over 30% from the previous year due to the tremendous stress on families. Mental health issues are plaguing society, creating traumatic effects on our communities. Hello global pandemic. Hello economic crisis. Hello protests and riots.

I am not intending to be negative. My point is that in these uncertain times, we are experiencing a plethora of unprecedented events and lack the coping skills to deal with them. The difference between civilization today and earlier generations is that we now have the internet and a non-stop newsfeed that amplifies what is occurring. Much of it is distorted. We are unable to discern that which is true if we do not take the time to check in with ourselves and *feel* how things resonate with us. Our ancestors may have known that a plague killed their neighbor but today we know how many people in our communities (and around the world) were infected, became ill, and died on a daily basis. We have to process all of this information at an alarming rate. However, we are not computers and we are clearly not designed to do that. There is no user manual broadly available on coping skills.

We need calm. We need calm to survive, to be resilient, to be able to cope and deal with life. We hunger for calm in our quest to rise above. Humanity needs calm to create and re-establish civility. Life is intended to be joyous and blissful. It's a challenge for many of us to be joyful right now. However, we must consciously and unapologetically choose this for ourselves. It's imperative for our survival that we re-center and move thoughtfully from our hearts, wherever we find ourselves at this moment. Both in big ways and small, we must reflect on where we are at this time. Current events are providing a giant reset which will certainly alter how we move forward. Many individuals were quietly relieved by a disruption in their life during the pandemic, despite the horrific news of death and loss, because they were simply able to stop and catch their breath. The art of retreating is about finding ways to stop and catch our breath, to check in with ourselves, recalibrate, and then return to our lives filled up with some fresh perspective. Perhaps we can be more joy-filled and blissful, have hope and faith that everything is going to be okay. Or simply be able to rise above a bad day. When we check in with ourselves and regain our own sense of peace, we can reassure our loved ones as well. A calm and peaceful demeanor is reassuring and can be contagious. Everything *is* going to be okay.

A CALMING EXERCISE

Take a moment now to attain a little bit of calm and centeredness. This is a great exercise to practice when something unexpected comes along or you find yourself in a heightened state of anxiety or fear. Sit comfortably on the floor or a chair. Close your eyes and breathe deeply and slowly two or three times. Feel your body relax into your breath. Picture a large glowing ball of light above your navel. Feel the glow of this ball as warmth radiating through your entire body and down into the ground. Continue breathing and expanding this feeling of warmth and light until it feels like it envelopes you. Now visualize a storm blowing by in front of you. Everything that is upsetting or disturbing your peace is blowing by you in the storm. The wind is carrying all of your worries and concerns. You can see them, but they are not part of you. They are just blowing by. Allow everything that is bothering you to blow by you in some form. Let all of it go. Remain in the feeling of warmth and light that you are holding at the center of your being. After the storm of all your worries passes by, notice how you are still there centered in the warm glowing light, undisturbed. You are unscathed even though you can see all the debris of your concerns blow by. Allow the storm to pass and return to the feeling of warmth within you. Sense how you feel after the storm has passed and remember this feeling when something else arises that disturbs you. Remember that you do not need to get swept up in the storm.

. . .

Morihei Ueshiba, the Japanese prophet of the Art of Peace (and the spiritual martial arts known as Aikido), promoted education and training in the way of ultimate harmony and absolute peace. Through repetition and practice, his students mastered the ability to calm the spirit and emerge victorious in any situation. He writes:

"Aikido is like an invisible wave of energy. The Art of Peace begins with you. Work on yourself and your appointed task. Everyone

has a spirit that can be refined. Foster peace in your own life and then apply the art to all that you encounter. Heaven is right where you are standing and that is the place to train."[3]

There is great freedom in moving from a place of calm, peace and centeredness. The broad field of options and ability to take action are rooted in terra firma. One is less likely to sway or bend to societal pressures and other external agendas. Freedom arises from discernment and personal choice to stand outside of the chaos that swirls all around us rather than get sucked in. Calm centeredness allows one to be the observer rather than the participant in the drama. Eventually the storm will pass by while one remains anchored and grounded to that still peaceful place within themself.

The great samurai warriors embodied the virtue that if you mind your mind, you maintain discernment which is a key life skill for all of us. It can make all the difference in a life-altering decision. It can impact the outcome as to whether you overcome a challenge, and build confidence and resilience during difficult times. Discernment reveals the truth to ourselves. It allows us to see when we are out of alignment with our authentic selves, our relationships, and our life path. Discernment

3 *The Art of Peace*, Morihei Ueshiba, Translated by John Stevens, Shambhala Publications Inc, 2011.

is a gift we can provide to others as well, through our example of service, care, nurturing and love. I encourage you to read about the strength and discipline of the samurai warriors. There is great wisdom available through the ages. I have personally been inspired and awe-struck by their rigorous training and zen way of life and have applied many of the principles to my own journey.

FIELD NOTES FROM THE EIGHT VIRTUES OF *BUSHIDO* OF THE SAMURAI WARRIORS:

One) **Righteousness** — Strive to do the right thing in every facet of your life. You can't control what others do or say but you have domain over your own actions and responses. Rise above and choose wisely.

Two) **Courage** — Be brave and feel empowered in the face of adversity. You have the power to overcome the challenges in your life. We are all stronger than we think ourselves to be.

Three) **Compassion** (my personal favorite) — With great power comes great responsibility. Show empathy and compassion in all circumstances. Give a hand up to those less fortunate than you. In order to help another, you need to understand their pain. Your act of kindness may inspire others.

Four) **Respect** — Listen and learn from another person's viewpoint and perspective. You don't need to agree or have to be right. There is <u>always</u> insight and wisdom to learn from another's point of view.

Five) **Truthfulness** — Be honest with yourself first. Be honest with others. You have an inner guidance system that helps you discern the truth in all matters. You just need to listen to that still, small, unwavering voice.

Six) **Honor** — Live your life from your highest self. Honor your own virtues and values and honor those who paved the way for your freedom, security and wellbeing. Honor the innovation and resiliency of your ancestors including your parents. Honor their sacrifices that were made on your behalf. Honor your legacy, and that of your children.

Seven) **Loyalty** — Form bonds of loyalty with others. These bonds are unbreakable. Be loyal to your mission and happiness in life. Be as loyal to yourself as you are to others.

Eight) **Self-control** — Mind your mind and remain calm. Calm is the secret weapon.

3

THE OASIS

"What makes the desert beautiful is that somewhere it hides a well."

—*LE PETIT PRINCE,* ANTOINE DE SAINT-EXUPERY

Last week while I was walking in the city, I overheard a father say to his children, "This is my oasis." He was sitting on a concrete bench along the waterfront. Now, this really caught my attention. As I looked around, there was litter and cigarettes scattered on the ground and the bench was butted against a low concrete wall. To any casual observer the spot would seem dirty, devoid of life, and absolutely mundane. But for this man, the location offered something to him. It was a hot day and he seemed a bit overheated as he sat there catching his breath. His two restless children were ping ponging off of the wall. It was the heat of the day, and the location offered no shade. I noticed that his eyes were closed. Certainly it was not the view that inspired him. The smell of exhaust from nearby fishing boats hung in the air. Yet, he had an expression of nirvana on his face, seemingly oblivious to his kids' antics. I imagined he was an out of town visitor who simply was looking for a place to rest. He had found his oasis in the midst of a busy seaport pathway.

Symbolically, the oasis represents *rest*. It is simply a place to stop and catch our breath. There is richness and fruitfulness found in an oasis. That is what we yearn for when the body, mind and spirit are depleted. It does not have to be a physical destination but it certainly is a state of *being* to which we aspire. For each of us walking our unique path, we are searching for that which uniquely quenches our thirst. It is not the same for you as it is for me. Our needs are different, therefore we will not find a *one size fits all* destination.

When I think about an oasis, the image of emerald green vibrancy and turquoise blue waters come to mind. The scenery of the oasis is enhanced with the sounds of birds and flowing water. An oasis is lush and bountiful. The air is temperate and cooler than the surrounding harsh environment. There is great sensory contrast and the ability to transform from one state to another in a place like this. I believe we find this oasis *inside ourselves*.

What should you be looking for specifically? Well, my experience has taught me that I'll know it when I see it. Further, it may not be something we actually *know* when we see, because it may have to be what we attune ourselves to through *feeling*. When you find your oasis, you will *feel* it because you will feel soothed and nourished. Something in you will shift.

The art of retreating is about finding one's own sanctuary; that is, peace and calm in the midst of life's unpredictability, particularly when we feel like things are out of our control. When chaos or unexpected events greet us at the door, we want to have our compass pointed in the direction of that attainable oasis. Yes, an oasis can be a place. I strongly suggest having a physical location in mind that is your reprieve from the world, but it can also simply be a state of mind that you can access through some rituals and habits that you develop in advance of needing them.

A few years ago, Madeleine, one of my close friends, faced a major health crisis. She believes that the condition resulted from the demands of building a business coupled with failing to practice balance in her life. In reflection, she states: "I wasn't finished yet and I wanted to be relevant and that's a tough and harsh benchmark to aspire to."

While she was absorbed with endless tasks to get her company off of the ground, she found herself ignoring her body's basic needs of nourishment, quality sleep and self-care. As she has shared with me in reflection, "There are different times in your life when the universe is telling you to stop and it slams you on the ground." This was not the first time she had been body slammed when her ambitions were out of balance with her basic needs. During those times she fought and fought against the warning signs, but this time she recognized them immediately and acquiesced to what was happening without resistance.

Madeleine's symptoms included a sharp pain in her ear that she described as the worst ear ache one could imagine. She immediately experienced difficulty with balance and was unable to walk with stability. She contacted her doctor who thought it might be a bacterial infection and prescribed some antibiotics. The antibiotics did not work and she quickly realized that she had been misdiagnosed. One afternoon after the onset of the pain, she found herself in the fetal position on a deck chair in the backyard cupping her head. Fortunately, a neighbor came by and found her helplessly lying there. Sensing an urgency, the woman pointed out that her ear was red and inflamed and insisted that she must make an appointment with an ENT (Ears Nose Throat) specialist immediately.

With some research and referrals she was able to obtain an appointment with a specialist relatively quickly, but as her condition rapidly deteriorated, she began experiencing some paralysis and drooping of facial muscles by the time she saw him. Madeleine was diagnosed with a rare syndrome known as Ramsay Hunt Syndrome. This ailment is the result of complications from shingles, affecting the facial nerves near the ear. In addition to the pain, Ramsay Hunt Syndrome can cause permanent paralysis of the facial muscles and hearing loss in the affected ear, as well as inflammation in the brain. The doctor put her on a protocol of heavy steroids, antiviral medication and Vicodin for the pain. Madeleine was indeed experiencing some inflammation and her doctor informed her that the nerves were so inflamed that they were impinging on the foramen of the skull and if the swelling did not subside, he would have to make an incision in the skull to ease the pressure. Now the possibility of having brain surgery was looming over her as well.

The immediate onset of symptoms left it nearly impossible to participate in her daily routine as she had done for so many years. The roles she played as mother and wife, business owner, athlete, social butterfly, and gardening enthusiast peeled away from her. Her healing required long hours of rest, solitude and a reprieve from all forms of electronic devices, family engagement, and household activities.

In place of her very full days, she developed a slower pace that included deep sleep, meditation, gentle yoga poses, and quiet moments in her garden. She surrendered all of her responsibilities and allowed others to support her and do what she could no longer do for herself. The intentional act of surrendering was a choice. She surrendered attachment to any form of guilt that one might feel by "checking out of their life." She recognized that this was a critical time, a seminal moment that she needed to pay attention to.

She recalls an afternoon when her sister brought her some touchstones, each engraved with a word: LOVE, PEACE, RELAX. She found herself sitting in her garden reflecting on those words. As she recalls:

"My yard became my ashram. I remember looking at one of the large pine trees in my yard and thinking that tree is not trying to be friendly, or boastful or cool. That tree isn't trying to be *relevant*. That tree is just being that tree in all of its splendid glory."

Then she quoted Lao Tzu :

Care about what other people think and you will always be their prisoner.

Madeleine constructed a sanctuary around herself cultivating the optimal conditions for healing to slowly take place little by little. Over the course of six months, she was brutally honest with herself and through love and forgiveness, worked on the parts of herself that needed to be healed. Through journaling and medi-tation the answers came. The insight came....**be still, and know**. In prayer, you are talking to God, however, in meditation God is talking to you. "I needed to take responsibility for my actions. This didn't *happen* to me, I needed to understand what was my part in all of it."

Occasionally Madeleine emerged and stepped back out into her former world and found it to be too much. She would quickly withdraw into the zen environment that had best supported her during the six months of recovery. Noise in particular was daunting for her to process, leaving her depleted and exhausted. Overall, it was not a straightforward journey, but eventually with her inner guidance and intuition she recalibrated through one of the most challenging experiences of her life. In place of her old habits that no longer served her, she developed a new set of tools, rituals, and practices that continue to sustain her to this day. She also added humor to her healing protocol because she understood that laughing engaged all of the facial muscles and therapeutically countered the paralysis and drooping of her face. Lightening up and laughing ensured that she no longer took herself so seriously. When her doctor saw her he said: "I cannot believe how much better you look!", to which she replied: "Laughter is my secret weapon! You should add it to all of your patient's protocols."

Recently, as Madeleine and I sat in the same garden that nursed her back to health, I noted how vibrant and peaceful she seemed that afternoon. I ask her what wisdom she can share from her experience that can help support others. In a relaxed manner she pulls her head back and gazes up towards the sky as if to reflect on my question. I know that she already has the answer to my question.

> *Allow yourself the time.*
>
> *Women are constantly guilting themselves and not allowing themselves to just be.*
>
> *When faced with a situation such as this, it's an opportunity to surrender.*
>
> *Be still and know.*
>
> *Acceptance is a big part of the healing process.*
>
> *It's an inside job.*

It's clear to me that Madeleine understands how her former choices and perspective on life created the circumstances for her to be slammed to the ground by the universe once again. However, she took responsibility and made the wise choice to create an oasis which would allow space and freedom to do the work to heal on so many levels. This sanctuary protected her from everything that was adversely impacting her health and wellbeing. She experienced a long journey which required her to surrender expectations about a timeline or a specific outcome.

In gratitude, she reassured herself that she was so lucky to have avoided a stroke, to have an early and accurate diagnosis. She convinced herself that she would never allow this to happen again. As we enjoyed the warm summer afternoon in the bounty of her garden, I note how confident and alive she appears while sipping her tea. Just beyond where she sat, I notice the trunk of the towering pine tree and its vibrant canopy that she had described. She is just splendidly being Madeleine in all of her glory, just like that tree.

· · ·

Sometimes, life comes in on us all at once. If an individual is going through a traumatic loss of a loved one or is working on the front line at an emergency room treating patients during the pandemic, different tactics may be needed to create some immediate relief. Intense pain is a red flag and may cause severe trauma with lasting effects. Professional support is always recommended first and foremost. Those with experience in navigating trauma should be primary resources for help and guidance. In conjunction with professional support, there may be little things that you can do for yourself to alleviate some of what you're feeling and to support the journey. For example, a power nap or hydrotherapy may provide immediate relief for an individual dealing with trauma. I often refer to this as *changing the channel*. Napping, as discussed earlier, disconnects us from consciousness and a looping mind. It also provides much needed rest when we are depleted. Hydrotherapy returns us to the state of being in the womb. Warm water baths supplemented with magnesium soothe a tense body and relax the mind. Studies show that the use of essential oils can further enhance our state of being and quickly reduce many maladies including stress, headaches, fear, heartache, and other physical, emotional, and mental ailments.

It's very important to note here that mental health issues, depression, and insomnia are serious matters that should be dealt with head on when symptoms arise. The onset of any of these conditions can lead to further health-related problems such as addictions, obesity and even suicide. If you are experiencing any of these conditions, you should not go it alone. There is a vast community of practitioners that can offer immediate help including doctors, therapists, and other healthcare providers. If possible, seek an integrative approach treating the whole body, mind, and spirit. If you feel the onset of any symptoms of depression, seek help immediately. I've provided some basic references in the resource guide and field notes of Chapter 12 and urge you to research practitioners in your area.

Over the past three to four years, I have developed my own set of rituals which define the art of retreating that work for me. Like many people, I have been dealing with an extraordinary amount of stress brought on by the ups and downs of caring for a loved one with dementia. My father was officially diagnosed in 2016 by a neurologist in Memphis, Tennessee. My mother had passed away in 2010 at the age of seventy-one from a rare form of small intestine cancer. She was diagnosed in the early spring of that year and passed a few days before Christmas. Without my mother, my father was all alone, void of family support where he lived.

My father is a brilliant man and was a prominent engineer in fire protection back in the 1960s and '70s. He created sprinkler systems that are used globally today. He was amazingly conversant regarding quantum physics, astronomy, politics, religion, philosophy and many other subjects. He also wrote Haiku poetry. He has been a dedicated, loving husband and father to his four children.

I adore him and so unquestionably it was an easy *yes* for me when he asked me to be the co-trustee of his will and trust, as well as durable power of attorney over financial and health matters. While I often say; "I didn't sign up for this," the opposite was true here. *Literally*, I did sign up for this. I just didn't have a clear comprehension of what it would all entail. There have been a lot of surprises and challenges along the way, and I have called upon my superhero powers more times than I can count, in addition to the love and support of my siblings, husband, and children. My father has two amazing caregivers named Ashley and Lillian who have personally sacrificed to be part of our family and team for my dad's care.

Creating an oasis for myself resulted directly from the stresses and overcommitment I have experienced in the past few years as a result of my role of caregiver to my father. In addition to moving him from Memphis to San Diego, I have been responsible for his medical care, his financial affairs, and everything in between. That is layered on my pre-existing life of working full time as an Operations Director, managing my own family's affairs, dealing with crisis management and transition for a number of family members who have needed support in the past decade, and trying to maintain balance and care for myself. Sometimes it's flat-out survival and sanity that I am grasping for.

Recently, in an attempt to simplify and streamline my life, I also made a very big move. After twenty-five years, my husband and I moved from a four-bedroom house to a 1,600 square foot condo. We shed most of our possessions to make more room for joy, simplicity and free time. From the outside looking in, it may appear that we moved far too rapidly with these life altering decisions. Our friends were shocked. Our children thought we were having a midlife crisis. But for us, it was the right move at the right time.

In looking back, the move was like severing appendages we no longer needed, in order to be agile and vital. By moving forward, paradoxically, we were retreating. One of my life mottos has been: **The more you have, the more you have to take care of.** In this season of life, it is far more essential to take care of myself, my family, and in particular my father, than to manage a huge household with lots of moving parts. There may be a time when we will want another house, but for now this 1,600 square feet is the space that I am blessed to call my sanctuary.

If you are reading this, I suspect that a part of you is also in search of your oasis or sanctuary. There are certain aspects of your life that may be filling you up and others that are draining you physically, mentally or emotionally. I invite you to make a list of both of these things. What most fills you up? What most drains you? Chances are that some of the things that drain you are outside of your control. When we are experiencing pressures that are outside of our control or influence, the only thing we *can* do is tweak what is within our control to relieve some of the stress and pressure. We can remove nonessential tasks from our plate. It's even better if we can replace energy draining experiences with things that truly fill us up. I refer to this concept as *"less this/more that"*. For example, when I was doing professional organizing for a living, my website tagline was *LESS CLUTTER, MORE JOY.* This applies to everything. (Substitute another word for clutter......less drama....less overcommitment.....

less spending....less judgment....less confrontation.... less self-doubt....and so on).

Throughout this section, the oasis is a metaphor to describe a refuge or relief from something difficult or unpleasant. Our shared humanity means that we all have unavoidable experiences that fit within this category. You may be thirsting for life quenching alternatives to the depletion and exhaustion left in their wake. Although you are on your own journey, I hope it is helpful to have a guide to help you chart your path along the way. That is what this field guide is meant to be. If you are well equipped to navigate the journey and know the signs to look for, then you won't miss the well in the desert. You will find the oasis, sit in the shade, replenish yourself, and be able to take life-affirming steps again. You will experience calm and peace, even if it is just for a short while.

In the following section, we will be introducing the field guide and pointing out the very adaptable and practical things you can undertake to retreat from the challenges, obstacles, and busyness of life. Each chapter is devoted to a unique habit or ritual that has worked best for myself and others I know who have sought solace in their lives. These practices are helpful things to do during times of chaos, transition, crisis, illness, overcommitment, and even just the everyday demands of life. I hope you will join us on the journey and find benefits from this field guide again and again.

When one thing does not work, there are half a dozen others to try. May this guide elevate your heart, lift your spirit, and point you and your loved ones to the north star of your divine health and wellness!

FIELD NOTES FOR FILLING UP AND LIGHTENING THE LOAD

Take out a blank piece of paper and draw a line down the center, top to bottom.

Label Column One: *Things that Fill Me Up*

Label Column Two: *Things that Deplete Me*

Brainstorm and list everything you can possibly think of that fills you up in this season of your life in column one. If you have to use both sides of the paper, by all means, do. If you are compelled to add another sheet of paper, go for it.

Next, brainstorm and list everything you can possibly think of that depletes you in this season of your life in column two. If you have to use both sides of the paper, keep going. Keep adding to the list until nothing else comes to mind.

Next, look over the two lists you just made. Is one list longer than the other? (There is no right or wrong here). This is a non-judgmental exercise. Just notice. Are you presently more weighted towards things that fill you up or deplete you? The comparative columns provide a good visual indication of where you are in the balance of your life right now.

Next, review column two and put a line through anything that is currently outside of your absolute control. An example of this is: My best friend was diagnosed with breast cancer, or I lost my job due to company layoff.

Why are we crossing the uncontrollable off our list? While these depleting experiences are definitely taking their toll on us energetically, we cannot change them. We can only change how we respond to them. There is a symbolic lessening of the load by crossing them off, understanding we cannot make them go away. When I do this exercise, I actually envision myself hanging from a cliff with a giant bag of rocks on my back...each rock represents events or circumstances that I have no control over but am shouldering as heavy worries. I picture myself simply dropping the bag from my back and watching it fall far below. This visualization serves to lighten the load of my mind when I worry too much, always offering relief.

You can do this valuable exercise at any point in your life. You most likely will find that the items you write down will change each time you do it. What we worry about today may be resolved tomorrow and part of our building blocks of inner resilience for the future.

THE FIELD GUIDE

4

THE OASIS FIELD GUIDE

"This is your journey, your body, your mind, and your spirit. Dig deep, own it and start doing things for you and by you."
—ANONYMOUS

Field guides have been around for well over 100 years. The first known field guide was published in 1890 entitled *Birds through an Opera-Glass* by Florence Merriam[4]. It described 70 living birds observed in the field. In modern times, there are field guides for all sorts of things including frogs, shells and weather. A field guide is a reference book intended to identify wildlife or other objects of natural occurrence. The

4 *Birds through an Opera-Glass* by Florence Merriam

common thread of all field guides is that they are designed to assist navigation and identification of very specific elements that are recognizable in the field. What distinguishes field guides from other types of reference books is that they are conveniently portable to pack along for the journey.

Field guides may also be people. These individuals are highly knowledgeable in the history and specific aspects of a place. Their role is to familiarize their audience with the details and unique attributes of locations, as well as the sacred and awe inspiring elements that might otherwise be missed. When my husband and I travel, we typically hire a local field guide to explore intimately what we would certainly miss on our own. Our journeys have included guided tours of glaciers, coral reefs, remote canyons, and many other experiences that would not be as memorable or enriching without an expert guide.

The oasis field guide sort of works this way as well. This field guide is distinctly designed to support you on your journey of retreat: introducing and identifying the optimal elements and rituals of restoring a sense of peace and calm. Without a guide, you may miss something essential, or lose your way all together. Innately we all know deep down what to do, but when we are swept up in life's current, our inner guidance may not get implemented. When the water is rising, we are focused on keeping our head above it. When the rapids appear, we are ensuring the boat remains upright and hoping that we do not fall out. A guide knows in advance where the smooth calm waters flow and will ensure that you see the beautiful birds in the trees along the banks or the deer feeding by the water's edge. A guide will say, "Look up!" or "Don't miss this." They have taken the journey many times before and can anticipate the twists and turns, the rough terrain, and the hazards obstructing the path. It can be exhilarating to ride the rapids if you're being guided by an expert. Joy and excitement replace fear. Whether the journey is downriver, or to the top of Mt. Everest, or across the Sahara on a camel's back, there is awe and magnificence to be revealed provided we are focused on the right things.

Metaphorically, field guides are beneficial in an ongoing process of self-improvement and knowledge enhancement. Our journeys may be through a life-changing diagnosis, a divorce, or a death. Perhaps this is your first time experiencing something like that. Most people will reach out for resources to figure out how to navigate a difficult and unfamiliar situation. We are not instructed in any formal manner on how to deal with these challenges. When faced with the school of hard knocks, we typically turn to friends, family, faith, the internet, or local community resources and find our way as best we can.

Equipped with a field guide as you traverse life, you are able to take responsibility for your own continuous education and development. This is a very empowering process. It gives you agency. The more challenges you can successfully overcome, the less intimidating the unpredictable world around us becomes. Confidence builds. Our days become less daunting, frenzied and uncertain. Fear is extinguished and replaced with a sense of assurance which can bring peace of mind. When we don't have to constantly be on the defensive, stress subsides, and healing and restoration can take place.

What are the key elements of a good field guide? The absolutes include the following:

It illustrates and communicates the attributes of something you are looking for so that you know it when you see it

It is simple, straightforward with information that is presented in a practical, easy to use and understandable manner

It stands the test of time by providing enduring information that can be used over and over again.

In this guide, we are going to identify the most supportive and foundational elements of creating a sanctuary of self-care. Each of the seven elements are a pillar of strength for constructing optimal conditions for a healthy sense of calm and peace in your life. By combining all seven, you are establishing a holistic framework to build upon.

There is magic in the number seven. Historically, seven represents completeness and perfection both physically and spiritually. Seven has been tied to the meaning of the creation of all of God's things including continents, oceans, planets, and days of the week. The number seven is revered in many of the world's religions. It is not by coincidence that I have leaned on these seven rituals to build my own resilience and strength during difficult times.

As I've mentioned, there is an exhaustive list of tactics that can enhance our sense of wellness, but my goal is to focus on specific achievable rituals that, from my own experience, I know work. If I was to design the perfect retreat weekend for myself, the agenda would encompass and touch upon each of these through a variety of activities or practices.

1. Self Reflection

2. Slowing Down

3. Nourishment

4. Awe

5. Stepping Away

6. Body Tune Ups and Flow

7. Enrichment and Exploration

In each section of the field guide, we will explore one of the above practices so that they become familiar to you and easily identifiable. Each one stands on its own merits, but together create an optimal environment for steadfast footing on our journey through life. In conjunction with these seven rituals, I will discuss the importance of community and our collective experiences in Chapter 12. Lastly, we touch upon our intentions for enduring change in our lives so that what we experience and learn about here can be maintained. Oftentimes we attend conferences or workshops that promise positive benefits but when we put the theory into practice on our own, we find ourselves losing steam and reverting to our old ways. It is possible to create accountability for the changes you want to make in your life so that they stick, and I will share ways to do just that.

My vision is to help you create foundational, lasting change that you can build upon. On a broader global scale, current events do not indicate that things are getting any easier or simpler for humanity. In our complicated fast-paced world, it is *we* who must have the resolve to create the change by *changing ourselves*. With the disruptive act of standing still, we are declaring individually that we need self-care, timeouts, and the ability to connect with our inner resources to refill the well of our being. We are shifting the mindset of go-go-go and do-do-do to an energy of conscious recalibration that positively impacts everyone in our world.

I see this restoration project as essential for our collective wellbeing and that of our planet. Just think about the changes that took place during the Covid-19 pandemic. We have all heard the stories about the greenhouse gas emissions dropping significantly during our global shelter in place orders, as well as many other aspects of nature healing herself. The skies are notably bluer, bodies of water are clearer and animal populations are thriving in the short absence of the human footprint. In a relatively miniscule amount of time, Mother Nature caught her breath and renewed with vitality. This one collective experience demonstrated the enormous impact of humanity's actions in the world. Let's follow her example.

As evidenced by the planet, we too can heal. If we can shift the global mindset to embrace and accept the importance of routinely stepping away from the chaos and busyness of life and embody this practice as a social norm, we can improve the mental and physical health and wellbeing of so many souls on this planet. As John F. Kennedy stated. "A rising tide raises all boats." That is to say that general prosperity is best for individual welfare, or in this case, individual wellbeing is best for collective wellbeing.

5

SELF REFLECTION

"Reflection — Looking back so that the view looking forward is even clearer."
—UNKNOWN

Mirrors are powerful symbols of inner wisdom and self-awareness as they reflect the world around us, that which we want to see and that which we do not. The reflection can be either a scathing harsh reality, a superficial fleeting moment, or if we look deeply, a peek inside our souls. Ultimately, a mirror reflects the truth. We all have the ability to change something we "see" in our reflection that is not in alignment with our true selves.

There is a phrase attributed to Proverbs which states, *"The eyes are the window to the soul."* When I am tired or stressed, I typically avoid looking in a mirror because I know the image gazing back at me will have heavy, sunken eyes. If I am depleted, my eyes will betray me in a heartbeat. Do I like what I see? Of course not! That reflection is silently screaming at me to "relax, get some rest!" That is when I know I have let things go too far and failed to maintain my inner reserves. Visibly, the joy has been wrung out of me and all that remains are black sunken hollows. However short-lived or temporary, I feel as though the light and vibrancy has been extinguished. This is avoidable and over time, I have learned through abiding practices how to keep this from happening. I certainly know that I need all of the joy and light available to me at all times to be of service and do my best work on this planet.

While the mirror provides the (sometimes harsh) reality and truth, there are other forms of self-reflection we can depend upon for assessment, guidance, and alignment. *Alignment* is a very important part of the work we do because it is a gauge as to whether *the outside reflects the inside*. Introspection is the greatest tool I have come across for discerning alignment of your reality with your hopes, dreams, and desires. I believe that the terms self-reflection and introspection can be used interchangeably. When we are being self-reflective we are looking within ourselves to clarify our values, assess our actions and make certain that we are on target. Introspection is the examination and observation of one's own behaviors, actions and emotions.

Honesty and responsibility are two components of this work.

Some people believe introspection is too touchy feely, whereas I think of introspection like a compass. It's the central tenet of our navigational system to ensure that life is pointing us towards our unique individual north. It allows for us to refocus on the positive components of our nature and enhances our ability to understand ourselves better, including what motivates us. We are easily thrown off course by distractions in our modern world, getting caught up in things that do not necessarily resonate with our own values or goals. Introspection reminds us of what is most important and of value to us. This is a healthy practice for our well-being. The easiest way to be introspective is to ask ourselves questions. A sense of *curiosity* is an advantage for introspection. Think of this exercise as excavating for clues! In Chapter One, I cite examples of questions that are introspective in nature that provide an indication of how you are doing. They include:

What am I doing to take care of myself?

How do I start my day?

Do I get sidetracked easily?

How is my mood?

Am I getting enough sleep?

Am I exercising?

How am I engaging with the individuals around me?

These are helpful questions that you can ask yourself regularly to see how on track you are. You don't have to write the answers down but by simply developing a mental *check in* you can assess a lot. Keep asking the questions and follow where the answers lead. It can be particularly helpful to do this when you are under extreme stress. The answers may indicate that a pivot is needed...pronto! If you are not taking care of yourself, the answers may indicate that you are running yourself down. Rather than maintaining a *business as usual* mindset, which under duress can be detrimental, shift into an assessment mindset. By acknowledging these questions and answers, you can take immediate action to change course. Even one step taken can improve the conditions you are dealing with. Remember, *alignment.*

One of the most impactful introspective questions that we can ask ourselves is:

Am I letting matters that are out of my control stress me out?

How many of us have fallen victim to worrying about things that are outside of our control? (For the record, my hand is raised). Though we can't do anything about the issue, we worry and obsess about it anyway. Newsflash; the world is full of problems that are completely out of our control. Worry and anxiety will not change the situation, but they will change us, for the worse. We have to channel our inner samurai warrior and *mind the mind* to direct our energy toward better outcomes. From my own experience, this takes practice.

At the end of this chapter in the field notes, you will find a list of questions that are self-reflective in nature. Try your hand at answering those that resonate with you. Again, I encourage you to sit with the questions and see where the answers lead. When we go through different seasons of our life, we are dealing with different issues and experiences. Some of the questions may not resonate with you today, but at another time, may be very insightful. I encourage you to really think about the answers, and if you are so compelled, write your answers down.

JOURNALING

When I had my first child, I thought it would be a great idea to keep a daily journal of our days so that when she grew up, she would have a recorded history of her early life. As time progressed, my daily recordings shifted to my feelings, my challenges of balancing work and family, and the highs and lows of family life.

For more than twenty-five years, I filled page after page with my dreams and plans, daily reports on the weather, observations on the pets, the extended family, vacations, gratitude, illness, loss, inspiration, sketches, musings and current events. Through the ritual of writing first thing in the morning until three or four pages were filled, they did become the history of our life, or mine anyway. I referred to the time spent writing as my *holy hour* and seldom missed this contemplative time for myself. I found it to be richly rewarding as it would set the tone for my day. If by chance my schedule did not allow for writing in the morning, I would take my journal to bed with me and write before I went to sleep. Many years later I also began a nighttime ritual of writing down five things that I was grateful for. Even when I had experienced a bad or daunting day, I was always able to express gratitude for those things that were going well. Typically this helps shed a bad mood and reminds me how blessed I am before I finish my day.

Over the years, I filled thousands of pages with experiences in need of expression, and hope, grace, and gratitude for the events of my life. Ironically, my children were never interested in hearing about something I had written about them or our family. However, writing helped me to articulate a lot of the things I was experiencing, and probably made me a better mother, spouse, and person over time.

Journaling is an incredibly powerful tool for self-reflection. Not only does it allow us to express how we are feeling at a particular moment, but it also provides a vantage point to gain perspective after time passes. It is like crossing a bridge and looking back towards where your journey began. We can see how far we have come, the resilience and confidence we've built, and gain a clearer understanding of our own growth. These are things that we might have been unaware of as we set out on that journey, particularly in times of uncertainty.

As our lives change seasons and we go through periods of growth and challenges, journaling provides a safe and private harbor for enduring what we are observing and feeling. Inevitably those feelings are going to change, but while living through them, they can seem unbearable. Transitions and cycles of life can drain our energy especially during times of loss. Journaling gives a sense of purpose and structure to each day, by both allowing for the expression of what you are feeling and the setting of intentions for the day to come. It is a sacred act that does not need to be shared with anyone else, providing release and profound perspective over time. The practice of self-reflection whether it is daily, weekly, monthly or once a year, can significantly enhance the progression of your life.

As a form of retreating, journaling creates a calmer space for you to thrive in. Morning is the perfect time to connect to mind, body and spirit because the events of the day have not yet unfolded and impacted you. The day itself is a blank sheet of paper. Spending time in quiet self-reflection allows us to slow down and acknowledge what is happening in our lives. Introspection keeps us from being stuck in the same playback loop because we are consciously acknowledging the drama or the stories that are playing out in our lives. This allows us to take responsibility, accept, or change them. What a powerful form of clarity! Like meditation, journaling intentionally brings your attention inwards and has profound lasting effects. Energetically it centers us by providing a powerful means of releasing any negative thoughts and feelings. It creates space to focus on that which you have and are grateful for. With routine practice of self-reflection, we are less likely to be impacted by the daily challenges of our lives and feel like an unmoored boat hitting the rocky shoreline. Envision seeking peaceful waters and finding the calm in this beautiful practice.

Once a year, gift yourself with a beautiful inspiring journal. Many bookstores and office supply stores now have aisles devoted to a variety of journals and notebooks to suit every preference, as do the big general retailers such as Amazon, Target and Walmart. Many people journal on their computers. However, I recommend as part of your overarching goal of retreating to really unplug from electronics, which can be both distracting and emit unnecessary electromagnetic field exposure. In addition, I feel that something magical happens when you transfer your feelings from your mind and body through your pen to the paper. Like alchemy, this heart to hand to paper activity is a liberating channel of expression to let go of what you have been carrying inside.

Use the suggestions in the field notes of this chapter as prompts for writing if you do not feel comfortable writing in a stream of consciousness format. Approach this ritual in whatever way best suits your personality and don't be afraid to push beyond your comfort level of exploration. This ritual is for your eyes only. From time to time, I reflect on my journal writings of the past. It is inspiring to see how far I have come on my own journey of growth, to know that my dreams and desires are unwavering, my courage, grace and resilience sustain me, and that eventually everything works out okay.

FIELD NOTES ON SELF REFLECTION

A SAMPLING OF INTROSPECTIVE QUESTIONS TO EXPLORE

- What am I doing to take care of myself?
- How do I start my day?
- How do I get sidetracked easily?
- How is my mood?
- Am I getting enough sleep?
- Am I exercising?
- How am I engaging with the individuals around me?
- Am I taking care of myself physically?
- Am I experiencing a healthy perspective?
- Am I using my time wisely?
- Am I taking anything for granted?
- Am I thinking negative thoughts before I fall asleep?
- What worries me most about the future?
- What is the worst thing that can really happen?
- Am I sabotaging my health, welfare or wellbeing in any way?
- Am I waking up in the morning ready to take on the day?

- Are my actions endangering the health, welfare or wellbeing of any other individuals?
- Am I putting enough effort into my relationships?
- Am I living true to myself?
- Am I letting matters that are out of my control stress me out?
- Am I achieving the goals that I've set for myself?
- Who am I?
- What am I grateful for?
- What am I afraid of?
- What is stressing me out?
- Can I change that which is stressing me out?
- Am I grieving the loss of something or someone?
- What does loss feel like in my life?
- What makes me excited?
- What makes me happy?
- Who do I admire?
- Am I holding on to something or someone that I need to let go of?
- What matters most in my life?
- What do I want to explore?
- What am I doing about the things that matter most in my life?
- What sets me apart from everyone else?

- What are my accomplishments?
- Have I made someone smile today?
- What motivates me?
- What have I given up on?
- When did I last go beyond the boundaries of my comfort zone?
- How can I be of service to others?
- Who inspires me?
- What inspires me?
- What do I need to change about myself?
- How can I express more love in the world?
- Who has had the greatest impact on my life?
- What do I want to do with my life?
- What is life asking of me?
- Does this fill me up or deplete me?
- How can I learn from my failures?
- What am I most proud of?
- What would I like to be remembered for?
- How can I improve my perspective on life?
- Who makes me irritable and why?
- How can I see a current challenge in my life as an opportunity to grow?
- What makes me sad?
- What would I like to see changed in the world and how can I contribute to that in a small way?

JOURNALING PROMPTS TO EXPLORE

- My favorite way to spend the day is . . .
- If I could talk to my teenage self, the one thing I would say is . . .
- The (one/two/three) moments I'll never forget in my life are . . . (Describe them in great detail, and what makes them so unforgettable.)
- Make a list of 30 things that make you smile.
- Write about a moment experienced through your body. Making love, preparing breakfast, going to a party, having a fight, an experience you've had or you imagine for your character. Leave out thought and emotion, and let all information be conveyed through the body and senses.
- The words I'd like to live by are . . .
- I couldn't imagine living without . . .
- When I'm in pain—physical or emotional—the kindest thing I can do for myself is . . .
- Make a list of the people in your life who genuinely support you, and who you can genuinely trust.
- What does unconditional love look like for you?
- What things would you do if you loved yourself unconditionally? How can you act on these things, even if you're not yet able to love yourself unconditionally?
- I really wish others knew this about me . . .

- Name what is enough for you.
- If my body could talk, it would say . . .
- Name a compassionate way you've supported a friend recently. Then, write down how you can do the same for yourself.
- What do you love about life?
- What always brings tears to your eyes?
- Write about a time when your work felt real, necessary and satisfying to you, whether the work was paid or unpaid, professional or domestic, physical or mental.
- Write about your first love—whether it's a person, place or thing.
- Using 10 words, describe yourself.
- What's surprised you the most about your life or life in general?
- What can you learn from your biggest mistakes?
- I feel most energized when . . .
- "Write a list of questions to which you urgently need answers."
- Make a list of everything that inspires you— whether books, websites, quotes, people, paintings, stores, or stars in the sky.
- What's one topic you need to learn more about to help you live a more fulfilling life?
- I feel happiest in my skin when . . .
- Make a list of everything you'd like to say no to.

- Make a list of everything you'd like to say yes to.
- Write the words you need to hear.
- My Bucket List includes....

SLOW DOWN

"*Only in quiet waters do things mirror themselves undistorted. Only in a quiet mind is adequate perception of the world.*"
—HANS MARGOLIUS

"*To the mind that is still, the whole universe surrenders.*"
—LAO TZU

I believe that my generation and that of my children have completely forgotten how to slow down and just be. I do fondly remember times in my childhood when we would play outdoors for entire days, lay in the grass and stare at clouds, and at night look for shooting stars. That time, or rather timelessness, felt quite magical to me. I also remember periods of time as a kid where we were expected to be quiet and still in church on Sundays, or to take a nap at a specific time in the afternoon. Those times, in contrast, felt regimented and excruciatingly long. In order to endure my childish boredom, I would daydream. Now, in this season of my life, I long for periods of stillness and restful contemplation which come far less frequently or naturally.

Today, technology plays the main antagonist in the story of our busy lives and subsequent free time. We're glued to our computers, the internet, and smartphones. Our children are unable to even recall life without them. I remember hearing my parents and grandparents speak nostalgically about Sunday evenings huddled around a radio after dinner or gathered around a campfire listening to stories for hours. We instead detach from those around us and go down the isolated rabbit hole of the internet or the manic world of social media.

Technology in its ever-increasing expansion and ubiquity has us running to keep pace with as much information as we can digest. The consequences include expressions like 24/7, FOMO (fear of missing out), WFH (work from home), selfies, follows, likes, tweets, texts, emojis and a barrage of other distractions that tether us physically, mentally and emotionally to our devices. Studies done on the societal effects of our smart devices classify them as addictions for delivering dopamine hits to our brains. Although we can now monitor and measure our screen time, that knowledge does not seem to curtail the amount of time we spend staring at them.

For the record, I am not an anti-technology advocate. I have all of the requisite gadgets that most people have, because I actually love technology and well-designed products. I have a desktop computer, a laptop, an iPad, and an Apple smartphone that are all synced and "talk" to each other. How brilliant! I have three email addresses (two for businesses that I run), two Instagram accounts (one personal and one business), Facebook, LinkedIn, Pinterest, and many other accounts that I utilize frequently. All of my photos and music live in the cloud, and I stream television and movies through a variety of platforms for instant gratification and entertainment. In addition, like many people I have a smart home including a robot vacuum, lights, appliances, alarm system, and even a water leak detection system. I have a digital camera which also syncs with my computers and allows me to render professional quality photographs. I am financially blessed to have all of these things in my life and to be able to keep them up to date.

As I mentioned earlier, the more you have, the more you have to take care of. In this case, keeping up to date with all of your accounts, social media, devices, other people's social media, as well as the latest and greatest upgrade of everything takes its toll on your time, energy and focus. Thanks to artificial intelligence and algorithms, each of us is constantly being fed tailor made data that we do not have the time or the ability to digest and discern. Advertisers, political groups, "news" agencies, self-interest groups and let's face it, bad guys, know this and exploit us through the avalanche of information coming our way.

On top of the demands of our "normal daily life," the bombardment of digital information can have lasting effects on our emotional state, and quite possibly the outcomes in our lives. Research indicates that the impact of social media and surfing the web are creating greater feelings of isolation and exploitation rather than connectedness. Cyberbullying, incivility, and crime are prevalent. Our children and seniors are most at risk of exploitation. I imagine that is not what technology was designed to do. The vision was to make our lives better and easier, as well as create global interconnection. When it does do that, it is a marvel of innovation!

Technology is here to stay. As the problems and side effects of its use reveal themselves to an awakening generation, responsibility and accountability will hopefully increase. The problem is that the development of technology moves much faster than the ethical and beneficial rules of engagement can keep pace. Now we find ourselves trying to keep pace as well. We simply must create the discipline for stillness and unplug more frequently for our health and well-being. When we feel overwhelmed, distressed, and unable to keep up, these are signs that the time is *now*. Technology is not the only culprit. Other people's drama, unhealthy relationships, illness, financial issues, and crises of all sorts are the universe's way of telling us to slow down and be still.

It is becoming increasingly imperative to draw upon our own inner strength through *self advocacy* and decide when enough is enough. By creating opportunities and space in our schedules, we can bring more appreciation for what we have and manifest what we desire. In addition, we are opening up to guidance beyond our own thoughts or reactions to allow for the small, still voice inside each of us to emerge, that which has our highest interests in mind, that of our soul development. Collectively, we can all share in compassion for what we are experiencing on the world stage with the global pandemic. It is bringing about monumental change and knocking down social norms that no longer suit us. We have the opportunity to pause and reflect like no other time in our lives to allow wisdom to surface and to care for ourselves in new and more nurturing ways. We can be better. When we take good care of ourselves, we can, in turn, care for others in an elevated manner.

Slowing down entails stepping away from our usual routines and habits to quiet the mind and let go of distractions and unnecessary busyness. With that, we are unencumbered to rest, heal, and find guidance that resonates with our hearts. As in self-reflection there are many ways to do this. Included here are the practices of unplugging, napping, high quality sleep, quieting the mind and nervous system, brain breaks, meditation and breathwork. There are other practices to explore beyond these, however the field guide intends to provide a simple sampling of practices and rituals that work from my own personal experience.

INTENTION SETTING RITUAL

Daily intention setting is a powerful ritual that I was introduced to while on a retreat. The wellness center at Civana practiced a morning intention setting ceremony which allowed guests to open their hearts to the possibilities of the day. I found this ritual to be navigational towards charting a course both emotionally for the path of the day as well as for manifesting meaningful experiences that one would like to bring about. Doing this in a group setting lended additional energy and meaning to anchor the commitment to move in an intentional direction. Even when I was unable to attend the daily intention setting ceremony, I found myself practicing this ritual in solitude. I have carried intention setting further by writing my daily intention at the top of my journal entry each morning.

Intention setting does not have to be profound or ambitious to be powerful. Simple intentions can carry us through the day. Try setting an intention for the remainder of your day right now. Take a few deep cleansing breaths and think about a feeling or an activity you would like to experience today. It can be as simple as experiencing a state of peace or to be "rooted in the here and now." It can be more dynamic as being in joyful interaction with everyone you encounter or being unwavering in your commitment to let nothing upend your day. Intention setting can bring clarity and centeredness to a day, an experience, and especially to times of chaos in our lives. It helps to create a roadmap for our days and sets us on a course of positivity.

UNPLUGGING

"Almost everything will work again if you unplug it for a few minutes, including you."
—ANNE LAMOTT, *ALMOST EVERYTHING*

Perhaps you were enjoying a really great movie at home one night and all of the sudden your cable goes on the fritz and the picture freezes up. You may spend ten to twenty minutes troubleshooting it on your own and then call the cable company to see if there was a power outage or if other customers in your area were experiencing the same thing (collective experiences make us feel better when things are not going right because we know we are not in it alone). For technical service, you press "one" and may wait on hold another ten to twenty minutes. Finally, the technician on the other end of the phone suggests you unplug your cable box and plug it back in. That's it?! Seriously? Lo and behold, it works! I'm not sure exactly why nine times out of ten this little trick works but Anne Lamott's quote certainly rings true. Almost everything does work again when we unplug it for a few minutes, including ourselves. We have to break the circuit and let things reset.

Whenever possible give yourself permission to opt out. This goes well beyond junk email. By unplugging from anything that is draining you in any way, you are removing the seeping energies associated with it so that you can reset. When the draining energy recedes you are more apt to experience calmness. I encourage you to frequently look at the circumstances or things in your life and assess whether they deplete you or fill you up. If your answer is "depletes," consider breaking your tie to it. (See field notes for examples).

For most of us, it is difficult to unplug. Why? On some level it's FOMO, or fear of missing out. Maybe we feel isolated and lonely. Or we're searching for the feeling of being part of the collective fun. Even if we were not invited to the party, we can live vicariously through the carefully edited photos of others having a good time, can't we?

Maybe we are very competitive and don't want to miss vital information such as performance enhancements that may give us a leg up over our competitors. Or we want to be sure we get the promotion over a co-worker by being on our game. Keeping a competitive edge can be daunting and exhausting.

We may be a new mother and feel inadequate about our parenting skills including everything from breastfeeding, to baby food, to preschool. We compare ourselves with other well-meaning moms and feel like we might not be measuring up or we cannot afford to put our children in a host of activities or a private school.

Perhaps we are addicted to other people's drama. We spend time on the internet voyeuristically watching it unfold or worse yet, getting involved.

We could be in an abusive relationship and are scared for our lives or that of our children as we search for answers, resources, courage, or freedom.

Maybe we discovered that our spouse was having an affair through a friend or stumbled upon this fact through social media. We may become obsessed with all of the details that we can unearth.

Maybe we cannot get our feet on the ground financially or have lost our job. We are in relentless pursuit of work at any cost. Or conversely, we are working ourselves to exhaustion and can't seem to step away or break from the compulsion to get more done.

For some of us, we've just learned bad news about our health or that of a loved one. We are desperately searching for answers and a plan to make things better, or to make them go away altogether despite many factors being out of our control.

Perhaps we are caring for a spouse or loved one who cannot care for themselves. We have used up all of our reserves and depleted ourselves in caring for them. We desperately need resources but do not have the time or inclination to find them on our own.

Comparison, competition, control, calamities or crises, these are just a few of the common mindsets that keep us in the go-go-go mode and make it challenging and yet necessary to unplug. Metaphorically, unplugging is the decisive act of *cutting the cord.* When a child is born, the umbilical cord that sustained the child in the mother's womb must be cut so that the baby can survive independently outside of its mother. If the cord is not cut, it will naturally seal itself off and detach from the baby anywhere from two to ten days after birth. This is the natural order of things. The dependence on things outside of ourselves for our entertainment, sustenance, ego, and to exert control does not sustain us nor give us confidence. We can rely on these things from time to time, but it's imperative to center ourselves within our own power, agency and inner knowing in order to grow and live a fruitful life. Nothing outside of ourselves can do this for us. We can lean on others to assist, but it's essential to know that it is up to us to figure out what we need.

Once we can unplug and skillfully extricate ourselves from those things that do not fill us up or sustain us, we learn that we can survive and perhaps even thrive without them and we may even decide to permanently remove them from our lives. Our individual circumstances may just require a slight adjustment or a shift in perspective. When we evaluate our life through this lens, there are many things we can control including work that drains us, relationships that aren't life enhancing, and unhealthy habits. Also included on the list, but not discussed in detail in this guide are behaviors like addictions, destructive habits, and unsustainable practices. These usually require the support and guidance of professionals who are trained in dealing with these conditions.

When we unplug, even for just a short period of time, we reconnect to our inner guidance system and wisdom. We are recharged with energy and vitality. Unplugging, like self-reflection, offers us space for perspective and assessment. There are simple and small ways we can unplug every day and make this part of our practice of retreating for the betterment of ourselves and our loved ones.

Stepping away from electronics, news, family drama, work, children, and our myriad of daily responsibilities can be accomplished in small but powerful ways. Set the intention to remove yourself either physically, mentally or both by first *giving yourself permission* to do so. Our intentions are extremely powerful because they energetically hold space for ourselves just as we would do for another person. View this as an act of self-compassion and love.

Just as we start a diet or healthy eating regimen for a specific period of time, we can take a break from social media for a day or longer, or not watch the news at all if we are feeling stressed or anxious from what we are seeing. While we can't neglect our responsibility for caring for our children or work, we can make a commitment to give ourselves some time and attention in solitude, such as when the kids are engaged in a structured activity, even if it means closing the door of the bedroom and reading a book for an hour undisturbed. We can also commit to shutting the computer off in your home office at 5pm and doing a light workout or stretching as part of your transition from work to home life for the evening. So many of us are easily lured into working beyond eight hours a day because we are *available* and more work is now easily accessible from home.

I recently read a post from a business colleague who unplugged from her social media for a month in order to manage the stress she was experiencing from the polarizing posts she was reading. Prior to checking out, she posted a declarative statement on her social media and apologized to her *followers* in advance. She let them know that she would not be posting, commenting or liking for the next thirty days. I really applaud her for recognizing the need to step away and take care of herself. However, it still seems strange to me that we have to publicly apologize for not *showing up* on social media as if life depends upon it. Frankly, I don't think I would even notice if someone I knew took a hiatus from posting.

In whatever ways we can unplug and slow down, we are holding space for rest, contemplation and even self-discovery by turning inward. The extrinsic distractions fall away leaving the perfect environment for refilling the well. Deeper practices of slowing down are outlined below. Find small ways to carve out time and little by little extend these mini retreats as long as you can stretch them out to find maximum benefits. Know that even a little bit goes a long way.

NAPPING

As I mentioned in Chapter One, napping was a foreign concept to me until recent years. I felt as if I was going to miss out on something and given that there are only one thousand four hundred and forty minutes in a day, I never saw the need to waste twenty of them napping. Over time and primarily due to exhaustive periods in my life, I have fallen in love with the effects of a good nap. Too bad I didn't learn this earlier. Today many companies offer napping pods for their employees so that the body, brain and nervous system can recharge resulting in more productive, creative employees. The scientific research on naps is highly compelling. In addition, we are learning more and more about the link between healing, wellness and high quality sleep.

Naps are short periods of sleep, in which the brain does not reach a deep level of sleep. The benefits of napping include better brain function, sharper focus, creative and critical thinking, just to name a few. There are a variety of nap types, including the *new moms nap* (you sleep when the baby sleeps), and the *disco nap* for those planning a late night out. The nap that works best for me is the *power nap*. I define the power nap as roughly fifteen to twenty minutes, short in duration but delivering maximum restoration. You wake feeling refreshed. If I nap more than about thirty minutes, like many people I feel groggy and low energy. Then it's difficult for me to recalibrate and get going again.

I typically will take a nap if I have long days of endurance work, whether mental or physical. For example, I found myself napping each afternoon when my father was in the hospital last year. I was required to make many decisions that would impact the outcome of his recovery. Having responsibility for someone else's life is energetically depleting regardless of your attitude and approach. For me every decision was made with love, but there was a lot riding on those decisions. I try to put myself in my father's shoes and approach it from that perspective. What would he do? When I returned home at the end of these long days, I needed to disconnect from the intensity of everything that had unfolded during the hours in the hospital. I would change my clothes and put my head down on the pillow for a short bit of time. Breaking the "caregiver/ decision maker circuit" and separating from the day's activities allowed me rest and recharge for what was to come the following day. It also allowed me to be more present for my husband rather than being exhausted and needy, and for him to be present for me.

HIGH QUALITY SLEEP

"Every soul needs rest, high quality sleep and stillness. The answers we seek never come when the mind is busy or overloaded."
—LEON BROWN

If you search the keyword 'sleep' on Amazon, more than 200,000 products pop up. As a sleep deprived society, we are in pursuit of good quality sleep, not unlike the demand for high performance products and services. Just a sampling of products include books, supplements, masks, sleep sensors, pillows, sheets, and ambient sound for our sleeping environment. In 2016, Arianna Huffington released the book *The Sleep Revolution* after her own personal crisis with sleep deprivation which caused her to black out and led to a traumatic head injury. Her book claims that we are in a collective sleep deficit crisis requiring no less than a revolution to remedy the situation.

With all of the scientific study and focus on the importance of sleep for both our minds and bodies, sleep quite frankly remains a more mysterious and elusive activity than other physical needs such as eating and hydrating. What scientists have learned through examination and clinical studies is that the benefits to *high quality sleep* are profound, particularly for our brain function and nervous system. The process of sleep is the most restorative action we can participate in for our overall well-being. Yet so many of us are sleep deprived or not experiencing high quality sleep when we do rest. So why is that the case?

Once again, technology is a contributing factor. Whereas our ancestors rested when darkness fell, modern society is lit up well after sundown, creating artificial cues that can manipulate our circadian rhythms of rest and wakeful periods. Lights in general after sundown disrupt our ability to get a good night's sleep. It is simply harder for us to unplug from lights, televisions, computers and smartphones. There is compelling evidence that blue wavelengths of light which emanate from our devices disrupt the natural ability for the body to sleep. Exposure to blue light or any light at all for that matter, suppresses the production of melatonin which helps regulate our sleep.

Because of these factors, when we do fall asleep it becomes more difficult to stay in a deep sleep (which is the phase where the restorative healing of the body takes place). How many people have observed their children (or themselves for that matter) taking their smart devices to bed and waking up and checking them in the middle of the night? Unless a family member is an essential worker or in the military, or is suffering some sort of crisis, it seems reasonable that we can wait until the morning to check our messages. I urge you to make a habit of moving devices out of the bedroom wherever possible.

Other major lifestyle factors that directly contribute to sleep deprivation are caffeine, alcohol and sugar. Caffeine can wreak havoc on our sleep cycle because it is commonly used to artificially manipulate our mental state and counteract fatigue throughout the day. Because it is a potent stimulant it can be significantly disruptive to our circadian rhythms as well. Each person tolerates caffeine differently. If I have more than two cups of coffee a day, I will get shaky and experience a rapid heartbeat. I also cannot have caffeine after 4pm or I will not be able to fall asleep. In general, caffeine consumption should be limited and cutoff by afternoon to mitigate any potential effects on sleep quality.

As with caffeine, alcohol can also disrupt sleep cycles. While in some cases alcohol can make us drowsy and fall asleep faster, it likewise can interrupt circadian rhythms, inhibit the deep REM sleep and aggravate breathing problems because of the relaxing effect it has on the muscles in the throat. Sugar is a stimulant to our nervous system and high glycemic levels cause us to sleep less deeply and display greater restlessness at night. When I learned this many years ago, I gave up that nightly bowl of ice cream that I so loved. Hormone imbalances and changes also can interfere with sleeping patterns and periods of deep rest.

High quality sleep is essential to our overall wellbeing and the restorative process of our brains and nervous systems. Sleep recalibrates our body systems including those of our immune and digestive systems, and it also provides optimization of our body's natural healing properties. Without an average of eight hours of quality sleep per night, there can be devastating effects to our physical and mental wellbeing and our ability to make good decisions for ourselves and others. There are of course exceptions, where some people require less than eight hours of sleep a night, but eight is the magic number for most people. It's very important to self-advocate for your health and ensure your annual wellness checkups include a discussion of your sleep patterns as a preventative measure.

I am a very light sleeper and have been sleep challenged for most of my adult life. I believe it is my 'ready for anything' constitution that keeps me from consistent deep rest on a daily basis. I have employed many suggestions and environmental enhancements to improve the quality of my sleep but have always steered clear of aids such as sleeping pills. My husband teases me about how many pillows I have tried over my adult lifetime. Melatonin supplements give me bad dreams which is a commonly known side effect. However, some people find them very effective.

I do, however, practice what is within my control including the following:

After dinner, I do not go on my computer or iPad unless there is an absolutely compelling reason to do so (such as an important work deadline). I used to read on my iPad in bed, until I learned about the effects of blue light on sleep.

After 9pm, I unplug from my phone completely unless it is to communicate with a family member or friend about something urgent. I set my phone for automatic "Do Not Disturb" with the exception of my father, his caretaker, and my children. I dock my phone on a charger in the kitchen and leave it there until 8am the next morning.

Around 8pm I dim most of the lights in my home or shut them off completely. We have also dimmed the display of our television screens so that they emit less blue light. (Most newer televisions have a setting that allows you to do this).

As soon as possible after dinner, unless we are going out, I get ready for bed, which includes washing and moisturizing my face, and brushing and flossing my teeth. I also minimize the lighting in the bathroom, signaling to my body that it is time to wind down.

In addition, I lower the lighting in my bedroom to provide cues to my body that it is time to sleep. I turn on a small lamp on my nightstand only to turn down the bed and write in my gratitude journal. I used to read in bed but now read on the couch and stop as soon as I feel sleepy.

I have placed light blocking shields over all tech items that are in the bedroom such as the smart thermostat and the remote eye on the television. There are no electronic devices on our nightstands with the exception of lamps.

I am a night owl and used to revel in staying up late into the evening well after my family went to bed. Now I routinely go to bed by 10pm unless we are going out. We also stay up later on the weekends and for special occasions. It has required discipline to do this but the benefits far outweigh the extra hours of wakefulness.

Studies have shown that the most restorative and deep sleep happens within the first *four* hours of going to bed which is typically 10:30-2:30 for me. Being a light sleeper, I find myself naturally waking around 3 or 4 a.m. I will then have what is referred to as a *second sleep* and log another 3-4 hours.

If I find myself waking up with something weighing heavily on my mind, I will pray, which for me means reciting a simple prayer of thanks for peace and calm. (For you, it may be something different). Most of what worries me in the middle of night is out of my control. I believe these anxious thoughts are simply suppressed consciously during waking hours and are looking for space to be expressed. I usually fall back to sleep in less than 15 minutes.

BE STILL AND KNOW

"Within yourself is a stillness, a sanctuary to which you can retreat at any time and be yourself."
—HERMANN HESS

Most philosophers refer to *just being* as mindfulness. Mindfulness is a fairly prevalent practice today, but for those who are not familiar with it, it is a practice of being fully aware of the present moment. There is an awareness of what is going on within you, and all around you. The key is to quiet your thoughts which is not always easy to do. *Just being* is a restorative practice which gives your busy brain a break.

Brain breaks are very therapeutic in times of extreme stress and chaos. This is a technique you can employ to *change the channel* in your mind fairly quickly. You can take a brain break anywhere, at any time. A brain break can be as simple as daydreaming or being aware of your surroundings. You don't have to *do* anything to just be. You just ARE. In the state of being there is no resistance. Often when we are in a state of stress or crisis, or anything requiring mental intensity, we may also be in conflict with something or someone, creating internal resistance. We find ourselves defending some aspect of ourselves triggered by fear, aggravation, pressure, loss of control, anger, or even survival. Taking a brain break from the situation, even momentarily, interrupts the energy of that state and shifts our perspective. I have often used this practice in times of crisis or deep emotional pain. Here is one example:

When my daughter was nine months old, we were playing on the living room floor and she suddenly had a seizure. She was in perfectly good health up to that point. Her pediatrician suggested we bring her in and within an hour of seeing her, he directed me to take her to the ICU for observation. In a panic,

I found myself nervously driving to the children's hospital while calling my husband to let him know to meet us there. This quickly developing situation was surreal and traumatic for me because I had no idea what was happening or what the doctor might not be telling me. Over the course of the day in the hospital, my husband and I stood helplessly by a tiny ICU bed as the nurses covered our daughter with electrodes to monitor her brain and heart. As I looked around the ICU, there were other parents hovering over their young children with the same frantic looks on their faces. I recall one baby in particular who had fallen in a pool and was on life support, adding to the emotionally fraught environment that we found ourselves in. Within a few hours of being admitted, I received an unexpected phone call through the main desk of the ICU. My mother knew where we were because I had called her to let her know. I heard her voice on the phone and she said, "I know you and Mark are going through a great deal right now, but I wanted to let you know that your grandmother just passed away." My heart sank as I heard this news. My daughter's middle name is Margaret, in honor of my grandmother.

The distressing news compounded the weight of anxiety that I was already feeling as I wondered what was going to happen to my daughter and whether she would be okay. At that moment, it felt like my life was unraveling.

In order not to fall apart and make things worse for my daughter, my husband, and the medical staff, I stepped away. I left the hospital and went outside as fast as I could, to escape what was happening. There was only a little courtyard outside of the hospital because it was in the middle of an urban area. In the courtyard there were giant pine trees and benches that faced the center. I sat down on a bench and looked up. The sun was shining and the sky was so blue. I smelled the scent of the pine needles in the heat. I took a deep breath and exhaled. I wondered if I had even been breathing before then? Suddenly I became aware of myself. I noticed that there were some birds in the trees. They were singing. They seemed happy and carefree in contrast with my own anxiety. The sun felt warm on my skin, unlike the uncomfortably cold temperature in the ICU. I felt as though I was being wrapped in a cozy blanket. Everything outside in this little oasis felt normal as if nothing was wrong. Nature was just going on with her business and I observed and felt part of it. Beside me, sat my husband. He had been there the whole time. Sitting there being present for just those few minutes allowed me to accept that everything was going to be okay. I needed to just be in that moment and take a break from the heaviness I was experiencing inside the ICU. Feeling better, we went back inside.

Thankfully, the health scare we experienced with our daughter was an outlier and within twenty-four hours our daughter was released from the hospital. She never had another seizure. We felt extremely lucky and blessed, and as we were discharged, I said a silent prayer for the other family keeping vigil over their tiny one on life support. I will always remember that moment in the courtyard. It was as if time stood still and everything I observed, the colors, sounds, and smells were so vivid. I became aware of everything outside of myself and created the space for the pain and fear to withdraw from my body. It felt almost supernatural. I was compelled to break with the trauma I was experiencing just for a few moments. I believe it was also the act of surrendering to what was. I couldn't change the outcome with my worry so I just had to let it be and let it go.

Brain breaks aren't only useful in times of pain and trauma. I have taken brain breaks when I just needed to put myself in a "timeout" from my kids when they were little. I have taken brain breaks in my bathroom and closet by closing the door, laying on the floor in the dark with my eyes closed. I have stepped out into my garden and watched the birds after receiving bad news. I have walked the trails of a reserve near my home after a bad day at work.

A great way to just be is to lie on the floor. It is truly a grounding experience to have the earth support you completely when you feel like you cannot hold yourself up anymore. I will lie flat on my back on the carpet or a yoga mat and close my eyes. It's even more effective and grounding when you can do this outdoors surrounded by nature.

Allowing ourselves to just be, whether it is the practice of mindfulness or simply *not doing*, is incredibly restorative on many levels. Energy is constantly moving through us and if we take a break when we need it, we allow ourselves to go *with the flow*. Our nervous system downshifts to recalibrate and fine tune itself. Emotions can surface and move through us with less resistance. Nature offers us wonderful distraction and displays of beauty to divert our attention from what we are grappling with. In this space, answers can arise to our questions and perspectives can shift. Make time to just be, every day.

MEDITATION

"Be the silent watcher of your thoughts and behavior. You are beneath the thinker. You are the stillness beneath the mental noise. You are the love and joy beneath the pain."
—ECKHART TOLLE

I have come to know meditation as the single most effective means of slowing down my busy mind. When I am able to practice meditation daily, my days flow more joyfully and have a divine rhythm to them. Even when something unexpected comes along, I have better coping skills and resilience on days when I have meditated versus the days when I don't. Meditation centers me. I feel that energy emanating from within me, and flowing out into the world, paving the path for a positive day. When I do not meditate, my days can be described as being a little bit rough around the edges. I find that 15-25 minutes in the morning is ideal for my schedule and my wellbeing.

Meditation is an ancient practice originating in Indian culture approximately 5,000 BCE. Various forms of meditation developed around the same point in history in Taoist China and spread to other countries in the Orient. Japanese Buddhism started there. Primarily an eastern cultural practice, it wasn't until the late 1800's that meditation was introduced in the United States during the period of transcendentalism. You may say that the West was late to the party, however meditation has taken off like wildfire in the 21st century and is broadly practiced as a secular modality of healing and mindfulness. Within the past decade, meditation has gone mainstream very much like its counterpart, yoga. Today, there are a multitude of meditative practices accessible to everyone. Meditation is now offered in company workplaces, at executive and leadership retreats, and even practiced by the Navy Seals for mindfulness and mental toughness.

While some people think that meditation is a religious practice, there are many forms of meditation that are secular in nature. By quieting our mind and attuning to our inner wisdom on a regular basis, guidance does differentiate itself from the external noise. People describe it as rising above the clouds, or as floating in the still waters below the choppiness of the surface. Meditation is a very personal experience that varies with the individual. When we explore and experience this practice, outcomes can include centeredness, calm, peace, insight, hope, possibility and trust in our own guidance system and the divine.

There are a multitude of meditation apps and an abundance of information on the internet regarding methodology. I have included a list of conventional meditative practices in the field notes of this chapter and encourage you to experiment with different forms until you find one or more that resonate with you. If you are a new practitioner you can begin with guided meditation to get the hang of it, starting with short intervals of time and slowly adding on. Meditation is most effective when you can cultivate the practice over time. Repetition and consistency are actually more impactful than the duration of time you practice each day.

BREATHWORK

"The breath is a bridge between the body and the mind."

—THICH NHAT HANH

Breathing is essential to life and comes naturally to us, so why would we include it in a section on slowing down? When we are stressed, we tend to have shallow, faster breathing, sometimes even holding our breath for short periods of time. Mindfully controlled breathing can be transformational to our state of being, influencing us physically and emotionally as well as our clarity and creativity. Amid the chaos, fear or confusion of life, breathing allows us to consciously open up like a door to let the silent wind of spirit sweep through us, cleaning out all of the debris and toxins. Focusing on the singularity of our breath is self-nurturing and provides an inner calm.

I personally became interested in breathwork about a decade ago while listening to some optimal performance recordings by Tony Robbins. Tony habitually practices a daily morning ritual of breathing called the *Breath of Fire*[5]. I listened to his guided instruction as I huffed along on my morning ascent up a local nature preserve. It was quite a challenging practice requiring

5 Tony Robbins Breath of Fire

endurance and fortitude to keep up! Over time, it became more natural and what was most appealing was the shift in my mental and physical state as the oxygen flow to my body and brain increased. Tony's breath of fire routine increases the body's vitality and is energy boosting, which we can all use from time to time, however there are other forms of breathwork that are more peaceful and relaxing, often paired with yoga and other mindfulness practices such as *Vipasanna*.

Like meditation, breathwork dates back to a centuries old practice in the Himalayas utilized by the monks and spiritual teachers. Known as the *Watching Breath*, this practice allowed the mind and body to relax to help the practitioner bring more awareness to the present moment. Today, breathwork studies show that these practices can significantly improve body and brain functions throughout the aging process with better memory, beta brainwave activity, and focused thinking.

We are ever-changing. Through focus on the ebb and flow of our breath, we come to understand how dynamic we are as individuals. Our breath comes and goes, as do our feelings, moods, and both positive, and negative, experiences. When we see the connection of our life force through our breath flowing in and out of the body, we can let go of attachment to outcomes and surrender to what is. Focused breathwork sheds light on our resiliency and ability to go with the flow. It's no wonder the expression *"just breathe"* is so prevalent.

SEEK SANCTUARY

There is a rebellious fascination and appeal to the idea of running away. I certainly experience the desire to do so from time to time and have throughout my life. Ever since I was little, the notion of hiding and not being found had a mysterious allure to me. I recall one occasion as a child when a group of neighborhood kids were playing a game of hide and seek. I found such an extraordinary hiding spot in the woods, that no one could find me. At first, I was quite delighted by my cleverness, but after some time went by and it started getting dark, I began to pout and gave up my hideaway. To my surprise, the other kids had moved onto another game and didn't even know I was missing.

As a teen, living in a somewhat hectic household, I often slipped away to remove myself from the noise and chaos. I craved solitude and nature. When I became a parent, I found myself dreaming of running away for short bits of time to reconnect with *ME*. On a few occasions that I can count on one hand, I was able to steal away for an afternoon or a weekend to unfrazzle myself from the overwhelming responsibilities of being a mom, plus having a fulltime demanding career outside the home.

I believe that we all are sanctuary seekers and have secret places in our minds that we feel can soothe all wounds and the wear and tear of life. Some of my sanctuary places included bookstores, the library, a favorite hiking trail, walking my dog, or just taking a drive while I listen to music. These are places where we *don't have to show up* for anyone else. They let us catch our breath for a little bit when life gets to be too much. In Chapter 9: Step Away, I will dive into this topic a little deeper, but for now, just know that if you feel like escaping your everyday life, you are in good company. Seeking sanctuary in whatever ways are soothing to you is a positive step towards retreating and restoring calm.

We've touched on numerous ways to slow down in this chapter. The practices outlined here are fairly fundamental and simple to adopt into your life. Cultivating the intention to slow down will make room for the space that we crave, desire and need in today's world. I believe that what we have experienced during the global pandemic reflects this as we reconnect with more simple pleasures with our families rather than sitting for hours of traffic each day. Breaking ties with the incessant go-go-go and do-do-do of life is like stepping off the treadmill that we have been on for far too long. Let's catch our breath, quiet our mind, and contemplatively reflect on our lives for a bit. Maybe it will help us all to be or do a little better.

DAILY GRATITUDE RITUAL

Just as we can practice a daily ritual of intention setting, equally as powerful is the practice of daily gratitude. Gratitude can bring clarity and closure to the events of the day, even for those things that were unexpected or did not seem to go our way. There are many gifts that our days provide to each of us. The more gratitude we have for our experiences, the more we are able to receive. Whether it be at sunset, or prior to bedtime, taking time to express our gratitude in the form of thought, verbal expression, or journaling, creates a reflection of the good things that are presently in our lives. By acknowledging and appreciating them, we expand our opportunity to recognize and cultivate more blessings for ourselves and our world. Just as with intention setting, practicing a daily gratitude ritual in a group magnifies the effect.

Take a moment now to slow down and be present in this moment. Put your hand on your heart and feel the breath moving in and out of your body. Thank your body for supporting you throughout your day. All of your body systems are miraculously functioning whether or not you are paying attention to them. Reflecting on your day, think about what moments, experiences or feelings you appreciate. Maybe it was someone that smiled at you on the street, or the unconditional love of your dog when you arrived home. Perhaps you received some unexpected good news or a friend or family member reached out to you. Maybe it was simply a walk through a park, or the sun shining today. Being grateful for all of the big and small moments of the day add up and give us grace. Notice how you feel after reflecting on the things you are grateful for. You will sense a positive change. Ending your day with gratitude rather than rumination can actually improve your sleep state.

I have provided some additional information on these practices in the field notes below as well as in the resources at the end of the book. As you begin to explore rituals that resonate with you, you may find yourself on an increasingly expanding journey of awareness. Experiment with what works for you personally and take time to develop habits for yourself. Little by little you will see a difference.

FIELD NOTES FOR SLOWING DOWN

IDEAS FOR UNPLUGGING

- Your smartphone
- Your computer
- Video games
- The news
- Binge-watching TV
- Drama
- An argument
- A bad relationship
- A toxic friend
- Complaining
- Judgment/Criticism
- Overeating
- Self-criticism
- Abuse
- Addiction
- Gambling
- Overspending
- Shopping
- Comparison
- Unproductive activities

- Sarcasm
- Fear
- Jealousy
- Alcohol
- Sugar
- Control
- Work
- Selfies
- Social Media
- Competition

IDEAS FOR NAPPING

Power Nap — set duration of time (set an alarm if you have to). Optimally, 15-20 minutes.

Cat Nap — short light sleep known as a doze. Can be even 5-10 minutes

Disco Nap — if you are going out late at night for a night on the town, an afternoon disco nap will give you that extra energy you need. Optimally 20-30 minutes.

New Mom Nap — if you are a sleep deprived mom (or dad for that matter), you can sleep when the baby sleeps to catch up on some rest. The key is to not feel the pressure to get things done while the baby sleeps, which can further deplete you and may lead to postpartum depression as well.

Emergency Nap — Feeling tired while you are driving? Driving while sleep deprived is as dangerous as driving drunk. Pull over (in a safe location) and take an emergency nap. Take precautions for your safety. Emergency naps are also beneficial in transforming an unshakable mood or looping obsessive thought.

Restorative Nap — These more intensive naps can be 90 minutes or longer and benefit those individuals who are shift workers that will do 12-16 hours of work at a time, or those dealing with crisis and trauma. While a full night's sleep might not be available to these individuals, restorative naps offer rest and restoration for the brain and body during periods of intensity.

Healing Naps — Sleep when you are ill. Your body and immune system need time to recover and restore the imbalances. Illness and disease are signals that your body is out of balance and your only job is restore order. Typically, the work to heal and feel well is completely passive in nature. You are providing your body with the optimal healing environment.

Lizard Nap — I love to sleep in the sun especially in my car on a cold but sunny day to raise my internal body temperature or on a towel on the beach in the summer.

I describe myself as a lizard basking in the sun. Lizards like to spread themselves out for maximum sun exposure. Just remember your sunscreen.

IDEAS FOR HIGH QUALITY SLEEP

- Set an intentional sleeping routine and follow it
- If you cannot remove devices, use the do not disturb function
- Dim lights in your home as it gets dark to optimize circadian rhythms
- Do not bring work into your bedroom
- Do not watch the news before you go to bed
- Avoid caffeine, alcohol and sugar in the evening
- Use blue-light glasses if you are doing computer work at night
- Remove as many electronic devices as possible from your bed and nightstand
- Eat at least 2-3 hours before you go to bed (the earlier the better)
- Avoid fluids right before bed - take sips of water if you are thirsty
- Go to bed and wake up at the same time every day if possible
- Take naps if you are a new parent or a shift worker to augment sleep

- Keep the temperature in your bedroom cool if possible
- If you wake up and cannot fall back to sleep, focus on what you are grateful for or say prayers
- If you find yourself obsessing or thinking about unnecessary things, try to focus on your breath
- Wake up to natural light and without an alarm clock if possible
- Optimal sleeping for your body and mind is 8 hours
- If your body clock differs from that of your family or roommates embrace it
- Wear earplugs if you are a light sleeper sensitive to noise
- Seek medical assistance if you snore or wake up choking at night as it might indicate sleep apnea or other medical condition

IDEAS FOR JUST BEING

- Focus on something outside of yourself
- Fully engage in activity in the present such as washing the dishes
- Observe anything or everything in nature
- Use your senses to notice everything around you

- Lie on the floor, close your eyes and feel the ground beneath you. Feel supported
- Listen to a piece of music in its entirety - classical music is a great sensory and emotional experience
- Take a camera (or your smartphone camera) out for a walk and see what captures your attention
- Listen to water flowing
- Observe your pet
- Do nothing

IDEAS FOR MEDITATION

There are a variety of different techniques to explore what suits you best. To follow are some suggestions. There are also numerous meditation apps that you can download on one of your devices.

Guided Meditation — A trained practitioner walks you through the meditation practice. You simply follow along. There are many styles of guided meditation.

Vipassana Meditation — Meaning *seeing clearly*, this mediation practice starts with focusing on the breath and progresses to observation of bodily sensations and mind observations.

Zen Meditation — Also known as Mindfulness Meditation or Zen Buddhist meditation, this practice is about focusing on the present moment with non-judgment and paying attention to the thoughts and feelings that arise.

Loving Kindness Meditation — Sending loving kindness to yourself and then out to the world through a set prayerful intention, you are increasing your compassion for all living things. I practice Loving Kindness Meditation every day.

Mantra Meditation — Repeat a mantra mentally in your mind such as *I am enough*. It is a powerful way of reinforcing the words into a belief through repetition. It can also be one word which carries a specific and powerful vibration such as *OM*.

Transcendental Meditation — a very popular form of Indian meditation with a component of Mantra meditation, this practice is used widely throughout the world with well-documented benefits. However, the practice needs to be learned under the direction of a T.M. teacher and usually costs money to learn the practice.

You can find many more meditation techniques through your library or an online search.

IDEAS FOR BREATHWORK

The Watching Breath — 4000 year old Himalayan practice of breathing that improves focus, and concentration. On the more esoteric sphere, it strengthens intuition, consciousness, and chakra balancing.

Alternate Nostril Breathing — Another technique derived from yoga, alternate nostril breathing or nadi shodhana pranayama in Sanskrit, deeply enhances the cardiovascular function of the body by lowering your heart rate. The practitioner will hold one nostril closed with a finger while breathing fully with the other nostril.

Belly Breathing — Belly breathing optimizes deep breathing by engaging your entire diaphragm. This technique is easier to do lying down on your back and maintaining the full expansion and contraction of your diaphragm within your ribcage.

Breath Focus Work — This breathing technique helps to experience the peace and calm that accompanies long deep slow breaths. When practiced for ten minutes or more, this form of breathing ultimately relaxes the body and the mind.

Lion's Breath — This practice is an energizing yoga breathing technique that directly relieves tension in your chest and face. By inhaling deeply through your nose and making a "ha" sound when you exhale, your throat, chest and face relax.

Breath of Fire — There are many variations of Breath of Fire, including that of Tony Robbins, which are for building lung capacity, vitality and optimal brain and body performance. These techniques stimulate the solar plexus and raise the voltage of the nervous system to a heightened state.

Resources for breathwork:
- https://www.goodtherapy.org/learn-about-therapy/types/breathwork#Types%20of%20 Breathwork%20Approaches%20in%20Therapy
- https://www.healthline.com/health/breathing-exercise#pursed-lip-breathing

IDEAS FOR SEEKING SANCTUARY

When you feel compelled to hide or run away consider the following:

- Your closet
- The bathroom
- Book store
- Backyard
- Garage
- Library
- Church

- Museum
- Gallery
- Park
- Trail
- Forest
- Garden
- A photo book
- A car ride
- A field
- The ocean, lake, river, pond
- An empty room at work
- A hotel or inn

7

NOURISHMENT

"Let today be the day you pay attention to what you feed your mind, your body, your life. Create a nourishing environment conducive to your growth and well-being."

—STEVE MARBOLI, *THE POWER OF ONE*

It is not just our bodies that long to be nourished but our entire beings. To be a fully alive expression of ourselves we must consciously, lovingly, and compassionately provide nourishment that enhances our bodies, our minds, and our spirits. I venture to include our hearts as well.

Over the past few years as I have become increasingly aware of how my mood can vacillate with the news and events of the day, I have developed mindful techniques for mooring and centering myself so that

I feel okay despite what is going on around me. This is challenging and I am not always successful, but I make a conscious effort. While I certainly want to stay informed, reducing my intake of daily information and limiting it to intentional high quality sources provides some reprieve and headspace to suss out **truth**. Just as junk food companies leverage our health and nutrition for a buck, so do most, if not all, media outlets. This is an age old practice that is amplified by the accelerated rate at how we now receive our news. Many people are unconscious of this and accept what they hear at face value rather than filtering information through their own inner guidance system. If we do not wake up and act with discernment, we are willing participants and victims in other people's agendas, which just may be to our demise.

In my own awakening, I have found it beneficial to create intentions that help guide me through the daily offerings of information just like navigating the aisles of the grocery store. We have agency and choice over what we buy or buy into.

Nourishment is this concept put into practice. Each month I choose a word that is a guidepost for challenging me to continually enhance my life and nourishment just happened to be my word for this past January. Initially, I wanted to nourish myself with love and self-care after the pace and indulgences of the holidays but the intention expanded beyond the basics (such as drinking 64 ounces of water daily) to a broader perspective across many areas of my life. Nourishment is the sustenance we ingest not only through our mouths in the form of clean healthy food and water but also through our senses, our intellect and our engagement with those around us. As I developed an awareness of this word and its broader meaning over the course of those thirty days, I explored how many elements of my life needed to be nourished to which I was not paying enough attention.

In addition to neglecting certain aspects of myself, 2020 literally got off to a bumpy start for our family. On a Monday evening in early January, I was attending a monthly networking meeting for a professional organization. It was a typical Monday, which can be rigorous, and I didn't even feel that compelled to attend. Ironically, it was the speaker's topic of self-care that motivated me to go. I drove over to the meeting and turned off my phone so that I did not receive any alerts that might disrupt the speaker.

After the meeting, I was feeling energized by the presentation, and turned on my phone as I headed to the parking lot. There were numerous missed calls, messages and texts from all of my family members as well as a local hospital. Immediately I knew that something must have happened to my father. I tried to remain centered as I headed to my car and began returning calls. I learned that he had blacked out while walking home from a local restaurant. When he fainted, he hit his head and was found unconscious and bleeding by a kind stranger who called 9-1-1 and ensured that he was transported to the hospital. By the time I emerged from my meeting, he was already at the hospital with my brother by his side. It was now after 9pm and I met them in the emergency room where he would be admitted and spend the next three days undergoing tests and observation.

My dad was not a cooperative patient and wanted to leave the hospital. He had been at this same hospital six months earlier after fainting at church, very much like this incident. Agitated, confused and determined, he kept trying to remove the IV from his arm as well as the electrodes for the EKG. The staff requested that I stay with him because he was not behaving for them. I spent three sleep deprived days attempting to keep his spirits up and trying to get answers to questions about his medical condition. Although the nursing staff put a recliner in the hospital room for me, there was no opportunity to rest because I had to keep careful watch over his every move. The minute I dozed off he was on the move out of bed.

The experience left me exhausted both physically and mentally. Compounded by the stress of not knowing why he was blacking out: I was constantly having to relay updates to my concerned siblings. Any reserves I had stored up were depleted in those three days. After he was discharged and I was able to return home,

I practiced loving and compassionate nourishment for myself until I was able to feel recharged and capable of resuming my daily life. Experiences like these are daunting and I am grateful that they only come around once in a while.

I certainly was not thinking about eating three nutritious, balanced meals over the course of those days in the hospital. I honestly didn't even have a clue what day it was. Hospitals have a tendency to be black holes of time. I do remember eating but have no recollection of what I ate or how often. I was doing the best I could under the circumstances.

When we are feeling emotionally or physically stressed, our digestive system can shut down making digestion and absorption of nutrients from food nearly impossible. This can compound the stress on our bodies and deplete our reserves for endurance. There are measures we can consciously take to ensure that we do not hamper our well-being and overly tax our immune system regardless of what's going on around us. This applies as much for *everyday stress* as it does for extenuating circumstances like what I experienced.

NOURISHING THE BODY

"What nourishes you is not the vitamins in food. It is the joy you feel in eating it."
—RAMTHA

If we want to feel well, we must nourish the body with good wholesome food that sustains our energy, focus and vitality. We optimize the absorption of vital nutrients by ensuring our bodies get what they need when they need it. There is a cause and effect relationship between our lifestyle choices and the outcomes we experience. For example, if we skip breakfast we will pay for it later with the effects of a low blood sugar crash. In order to nourish for endurance and negate the side effects of poor nutrition, prioritize and make a plan to eat well whenever you can.

Planning a basic food menu on a weekly or bi-weekly basis will keep you more on track with your goals than winging it. We cannot always be in control of our schedules, but with a menu plan, we are more apt to eat well and to be prepared in the event something comes up. Be in control of the food you put in your body and know where your food comes from. Advocate for your family's health and practice sustainable living by eating organically produced food as much as possible. Grow a small vegetable garden, even if you only have space for an herb garden on your patio or a pot on your kitchen counter. There is vitality and pleasure in the food you grow and prepare yourself. Good nutrition is essential to good health and wellbeing. Fuel your body for endurance.

When the stay at home orders went into effect due to the pandemic, there was a resurgence of cooking healthy meals at home. People are falling in love with cooking and baking again.

Some individuals are discovering cooking for the first time. My friends are all enjoying the pleasure of making bread and exchanging recipes! Know that pre-packaged food, fast food, takeout, and processed snacks and meals will never allow you to perform at your best. Take charge of your food choices by selecting food that is fresh, whole, and nutrient dense. Eat produce that is seasonally available in your area and try new recipes with these items. From Pinterest to food blogs, there are so many sources of inspiration available on the internet.

Hydrate with ample amounts of water throughout your day and remember to take your water bottle wherever you go. I recently found a sling that allows me to carry my water bottle hands free. Water and proper nourishment are equally important for the health of your skin, the largest organ of your body. When you start your day, prime your digestive system with a glass of water with lemon, or a tonic made with green veggies and fruit. Your skin reflects the effects of proper hydration and will look dull and flaky when you are dehydrated. It should glow with vibrancy no matter your age. Be mindful of the products you put on your skin which absorb into your bloodstream. Opt for chemical free moisturizers, soap, shampoos and sunscreens.

If you can only do a handful of things to improve your nutrition every day, I recommend the following non-negotiables to choose from.

Eat breakfast daily. Your body needs fuel when you first wake up. Ensure that you have some protein as part of this meal to balance your blood sugar level and to optimize brain function.

Drink plenty of water. 64 ounces, or eight glasses, a day. Begin as soon as you wake up. Do not drink a lot of water before bed because it will disrupt your sleep and also impact the slower digestive processes that take place overnight.

Eat various forms of protein including those derived from plant and animal sources. If you are plant based, try different grains and beans such as quinoa and lentils which offer a high protein punch and fiber. If you are nut tolerant, eat healthy nuts like almonds and walnuts which give you sustained energy. Walnuts have been proven to improve cognitive brain function because they have a high content of DHA, a type of Omega-3 fatty acid.

Lower your intake of simple carbohydrates, such as bread, pasta, and processed foods. Find ways to limit portion size or forgo them altogether. Focus instead on large portions of protein and complex carbohydrates like veggies, fruit, and whole grains.

Use supplements to balance your nutrition. The best source of minerals and vitamins will always be food, but for insurance add Omega-3-6-9 fatty acids, vitamins C & D which are beneficial to your immune system. The B vitamins are helpful for your brain and energy. Some people opt for a daily multivitamin.

If you can build upon the basics, here are some other ideas to incorporate:

Visit a farmer's market weekly or have a farmers market box delivered to your home. Find ways to incorporate more fresh vegetables and fruits in your daily eating regimen. You will also be supporting the local farm community where you live.

Try having a *free* day each week. Going meat free, dairy free, or gluten free even one day a week can provide a rest for your body. Elimination *diets* are great for getting to the root cause of certain health issues. For example, when I removed gluten from my diet, I no longer experienced chronic sinus infections. Some of my family and friends practice different forms of fasting or intermittently go on the *Whole-30* or KETO regimen. Experiment and find what sustains your specific needs.

Consult your medical practitioner before drastically changing your diet or eating habits.

If you are in search of nutritional guidelines during an illness or medical treatment, seek professional guidance from your doctor and a licensed nutritionist. This is imperative when you are taking medications that may have interactions with certain types of food or supplements.

During more stressful times, some basic things you can do to reduce the stress load on your system:

Reduce your intake of food containing animal products which take longer to digest. Instead, opt for nutritious smoothies, raw juices, and elixirs. The good news is these high nutrient drinks are one of the fastest growing components of the beverage industry and are readily available in markets and fast (super) food storefronts everywhere. Your digestive system will be able to absorb the nutrients from a smoothie far more efficiently than from a slice of pepperoni pizza.

Up your intake of Vitamins C & D during stressful times which directly boost and support your immune system so that it is not compromised by the effects of stress or lack of rest. Supplement as well with minerals such as magnesium which helps regulate sleep. Magnesium can be absorbed through the skin if you opt for an Epsom salt bath and has the dual benefit of relaxing your muscles.

It is imperative to stay hydrated. Although it can be challenging to stay properly hydrated on the run (64 ounces of water is the minimum daily requirement). Develop the habit of carrying a thermal water bottle with you. Empty or full, the water bottle is a visual reminder to hydrate.

Avoid intake of excessive caffeine and sugar. I discussed the effects of these items on sleep in Chapter Six. However, equally important is their adverse impact on your nervous system, increasing the stress load that you are already experiencing. Soothe and calm your nerves with a cup of peppermint or chamomile tea. I always keep both of these on hand. Peppermint is extremely soothing to an upset stomach and chamomile is a natural relaxant and can help to make you sleepy.

Eat slowly. Take time to enjoy your food rather than eating on the go. This helps your digestion and gives your mind and body a brief break from any stressful situation.

HYDROTHERAPY

For many individuals including myself, water can be very therapeutic during traumatic and stressful times. The simple act of taking a shower or a bath can briefly 'wash your cares away' and help you relax or shift gears. If you have a bathtub, you can supplement your bathwater with essential oils, Epsom salts and other minerals that nourish and soothe sore or achy muscles. I enjoy lighting a candle while bathing, rather than having the lights on. Lock the door and add a "do not disturb" sign so that you can relax in peace. Soaking in a tub is a sanctuary unto itself and a wonderful way to retreat from the world.

If you have access to a jacuzzi, this is another way to bring hydrotherapy into your routine. Just like a bath, the hot pulsating water remedies sore and stiff muscles, and increases blood circulation. Additionally, beneficial hydrotherapy is a steam room. A side benefit of the steam room is that you can hide away from the world! I regularly practice some form of hydrotherapy every few days outside of my regular showering routine. On my last wellness retreat, I adventured in between the hot and cold plunge pools which stimulate your nervous system, brain and circulatory system. It was an exhilarating experience and also got me giggling. If you have access to these types of facilities, mix it up for variation and different benefits.

NOURISHING THE MIND

We have a choice as to what to feed our bodies and well as our minds. Our mental vitality is enhanced with uplifting and inspirational content and dampened by a constant diet of doom and gloom news. While we strive to stay informed, we also must consider the sources of the information that we are ingesting every day. Our minds can be either a friend or a foe, so we must mind the mind.

Rather than listening to the news constantly, consider carving out some time for some soulful reading. I like to read inspirational books and poetry early in the morning during my *holy hour* because they transport me away from ruminating thoughts and generate new creative ideas and inspiration beyond my own little world. For me the subject matter is typically self-development, art and design, spirituality, cooking, and travel. For you it may be something completely different like historical fiction, biographies, scientific or medical advancements, or a mystery novel. Whether it's a book or a magazine, reading allows us an escape and provides the ability to integrate new information and perspectives. Whatever the topic, consider it *food for thought*. Remember, garbage in, garbage out, so prioritize high quality, uplifting material.

If you prefer television, consider documentaries and programs that teach you about something. My husband

and I will watch television after dinner and have a number of binge worthy shows that we enjoy, however, we also like to watch scientific or historical documentaries, as well as anything produced by National Geographic. Currently I am filled with inspiration by learning about the national parks that we have not yet visited, but plan to see in the future. Our Southwest Grand Circle trip of more than ten national parks and attractions was inspired by a Nat Geographic documentary. It was one of the most awe-inspiring trips of our lives.

MUSIC AND SOUND THERAPY

I find music to be a dynamic way to move energy through the body. My personal taste in music is certainly diverse ranging from Himalyan singing bowls and rain forest sounds in the morning, to Zen music during intense hours of concentrated work, classical music to stimulate creativity and right brained activity, Coldplay for running and working out, Diana Krall and Bossa Nova for preparing dinner (while dancing of course!), and chill, coffee house music for driving. I also listen to vintage Jazz, Hip Hop, and country. My musical tastes are as diverse as my moods and set the tone for the activities I am engaging in. My personal intolerances include destructive, violent and profane lyrics, and heavy metal which makes me feel drained.

Listening to classical music has great benefits such as lowering the body's stress response, improving brain function, and more focused attention. There have been studies done on the *Mozart Effect* which demonstrate that listening to Mozart's concertos for ten minutes a day may induce a short term improvement on task related performance.

A more recent trend which is growing in popularity is sound therapy, which is actually an ancient technique of healing. The Himalayan monks created clay sound and crystal singing bowls which they believed attune energy with that of the divine. Singing bowls are frequently used in conjunction with yoga practice as well. Today sound therapy practitioners as well as the number of people attending sound therapy retreats and sessions are growing.

During the pandemic, I have been gifting friends with small Himalayan singing bowls. Not only do they make beautiful sounds that emanate out into the environment, but they are little works of art. I like to believe they attune the sound waves of our home and have beneficial effects on all living things including my houseplants. For a few months after the stay at home orders went into place, all of our neighbors in the city would ring bells and bang on pots and pans at 8pm every night to connect with each other and pay tribute to our local frontline heroes. I tapped on a singing bowl with a wooden gong. Small but mighty, the sound from this bowl was powerful and loud. I encourage you to explore the world of sound therapy, as I feel it will become a mainstream modality of healing in the coming years. If you do not have a local source for acquiring a singing bowl, you can order one on Amazon. You can also find singing bowl music videos on YouTube and music stations. Singing bowls are amazingly calming and centering for the nervous system and transcend us to another state of being.

MEDITATION, JOURNALING AND YOGA

While I've already discussed meditation and journaling in the chapters on Self Reflection and Slowing Down, I wanted to reiterate that these practices are also incredibly nourishing for our minds and our souls. The process of going within and reflecting on our lives can nourish us energetically and spiritually like no other sustenance on this planet. Meditation is a direct plug-in to the main source of life energy. I mention both practices here as a reminder to engage in them as regularly as possible because of their infinite benefits. Yoga is nourishing to our bodies, minds and spirits, as well. The combination of these practices challenge us on many levels including balance, intention, flexibility, breathwork and releasing resistance. I will go into greater depth on yoga practice in Chapter 10 ~ Body Tune up.

NOURISHING HOBBIES

The boredom of being quarantined during the pandemic motivated many people to develop new hobbies and talents. We are reconnecting with simple pleasures that bring us joy such as reading, crafts, baking, and spending time in nature. I see the inspiration and silver linings in these activities and the human spirit pouring forth. Afterall, we are all creators and artists. For me, the hobbies I have reengaged in are painting and writing. I completed a large painting which is currently at the framers. I am also optimistic that I will finish this book because I have had uninterrupted time to write. I believe that hobbies are an integral part of our retreating rituals. Whether it is chess, breadmaking, gardening, knitting, drawing, model building, writing music, crossword puzzles or other stimulating endeavors, hobbies provide an escape and challenge us to grow. They also fuel and nourish our souls because they cultivate creativity and enrich our lives by pushing beyond the mundane and routine cadence of life.

NOURISHING YOUR HEART

While I am conscious of eating for wellness and fueling my mind with content that is rich in soul growth, development, intellectual curiosity and beauty, I have sometimes ignored the *nutrients* that my heart desires. I am blessed to be happily married, with two beautiful children, extended family, friends, community, and colleagues at work. However, sometimes there is a still, small voice that reminds me that there is still *something more that I want from life*. I've learned that it's essential to nourish your heart and follow through on your dreams and desires. Frequently we set them aside in order to put others' needs first. Unfulfilled dreams and desires can weigh heavily on our hearts.

We do not want to have any regrets when we leave this earth. I encourage you to build your bucket list and find opportunities to accomplish your dreams as much as possible. Whether large or small, do not give up on them. Life is full of miracles if you keep your mind open to receiving them. What might not be possible today may appear tomorrow just from the manifesting energy of your wishes.

As I was listening to a podcast recently, the commentator was discussing what most people plan on doing after the pandemic passes and we have more freedom to return safely to getting out and about. Among the most common responses was ticking off some of the things on their bucket list. With so much loss around us, people are realizing that life is short and it's important to prioritize what really matters. Our dreams and desires give us hope and pull us forward. I believe we are awakening to the notion that what nourishes the heart feeds the spirit.

To summarize, nourishment extends far beyond the food that we eat. When we do not address the needs of the body, mind, heart, and spirit, we may experience imbalances in other areas of our life. To nourish is to richly and lovingly fill up. It's like making a grocery list when you know provisions are getting low. Rather than deplete yourself, continually take stock of what you need. Is it rest, creativity, joy, solitude, balance, a lifestyle change, a change in scenery? Whatever it is, take note and restock.

FIELD NOTES ON NOURISHMENT

HOW ARE YOU NOURISHING YOURSELF?

At the end of each month, take stock of how you are doing in the major areas of your life. Where are you feeling depleted? Where do you have room for improvement?

Rate yourself from 1-10 on your physical, mental, and spiritual health. How are your relationships going? What relationships do you need to nourish and culti-vate? Are you tending to your heart through creativity, leisure time, and heart centered activities? Are you in balance with your work and personal life, your finances, your fitness and your health?

Taking a periodic assessment of these things can keep our attention focused on the instrument panel of our lives and ensure that everything is running smoothly. We cannot possibly put our focus on all of these aspects simultaneously, however rotating our awareness through each facet helps us acknowledge what needs attention so that we can implement a plan.

A few more ways to nourish yourself:

- Cuddle with a pet
- Change into your pjs when you return home in the afternoon

- Take walks in nature
- Cook or bake something
- Stretch on a mat
- Rest and sleep
- Bring home fresh flowers
- Have some chocolate
- Take a hike
- Watch the sun rise or set
- Observe clouds floating by
- Look for shooting stars and satellites in the night sky
- Plan a trip for someday
- Retreat for a day
- Go off the grid from family and friends for a break
- Go social media free for a day, a week or a month
- Rearrange and refresh a room in your home
- Polish up your bucket list and start checking things off

AWE

"Nature never did betray the heart that loved her."
—WILLIAM WORDSWORTH

Astrologically, my zodiac sign is Cancer, ruled by the moon. Among other personality traits, Cancerians are homebodies. Just like the crab, a person born under this sign is most comfortable in "its own shell' and feels best while at home surrounded by loved ones. While I do love being at home, I have an incredibly strong sense of wanderlust and spend an inordinate amount of my time daydreaming about where I will go next. I absolutely love to explore, and if it were not for budgetary and time limitations as well as family responsibilities, I would be untethered and on the go, exploring the world as frequently as possible. A self-described hummingbird, I need a constant change of scenery to fill me up.

Hummingbirds do not like to stay in one place and cannot survive in captivity.

The reality of life is that unless we are extremely fortunate, there are limitations to how much we can go off and explore. Our obligations such as jobs, family, homelife and community keep us tethered to some extent. Limitations include our finances, schedules, vacation time, childcare, pets, extended family, and whatever is happening in different seasons of our life. The pandemic certainly redefined where we could or could not go. But all hope is not lost, there are still ways we can safely access our sense of adventure to get out and see the world, with some modifications.

Over the past decade, I learned a very valuable lesson from my parents through the unexpected illnesses that they experienced. These events reaffirmed that life is very short, and we should not put things off for a future that may never arrive. My mom developed a very rare form of small intestine cancer shortly after she retired in her early sixties. Less than eight months after diagnosis she passed away. We were unprepared for the abrupt departure of her presence from our lives. Luckily, she had the opportunity to explore all of the things she loved including traveling, painting, shopping, creating traditions and celebrations for her family and friends and most importantly, being with her children and grandchildren. My father often says he is happy-sad because she did everything she wanted to do while she lived but her life was cut short. Thankfully we have beautiful enduring memories to carry us through our lives since she is no longer with us.

My father's life was upended as well. Within two years' time, he was diagnosed with two different forms of cancer, followed by the diagnosis of early onset dementia. We had to pivot as a family to provide support for his health and wellbeing for a disease that does not have a predictable trajectory. In the process, he gracefully accepted his fate and changed his plans to ensure not only his well-being, but that of his children. This included a move across the country and giving up his home of thirty-five years, his community, and a sense of a predictable life. Each day of clarity became a precious gift. Today, some days are unpredictable, unexpected, and sometimes frightening. We take them one day at a time.

Neither of my parents expected that they would be dealing with such major health issues on the heels of retirement. Who plans for a terminal illness or a life altering accident? It is not our human nature to do so. Life is so very precious, and we have no idea how much time we will have. I have come to the conclusion that we must live each day we have to the fullest for each of them are a blessing. There is no reason I can see to waste time or put off plans for the future. For me, carpe diem (seize the day) is a philosophy of life. Because of my parents' journey, I know how important it is to go live this life with wonder and awe, experiencing as much of it as we can while we can.

Last year while hiking in Zion National Park through the narrows, a challenging trek through waist deep water, I was amazed to see an elderly couple in their 80's wading cautiously through the water. They appeared to be in good shape as they carefully navigated each step. I felt so much appreciation for the journey this couple was making. How fortunate for them to be blessed with the opportunity to enjoy each other's company and the beauty of nature in this spectacular place. I pray that someday I will still be able to do the same with my husband by my side. None of us know what experiences lie ahead or how numbered our days are which is why it's important to prioritize our dreams and take steps to fulfill them in small and big ways.

This chapter's focus is not about regrets. Rather, it's encouragement for living life to the fullest with the precious moments we are given, by getting out and exploring the world around us. In nature and other sacred places, we experience the magnificence of the world beyond the threshold of our lives and partake in the wonder and awe of this planet. These activities are accessible to us every single day. We do not have to plan an elaborate trip to experience wonder and awe. With a little planning and attention, they are within our grasp in many different forms. In addition, these practices are undoubtedly good for our mental health and overall well-being.

WANDER OFTEN

The beauty of a change of scenery is that it provides a new perspective. Whether it's walking on the beach, hiking through a lush green forest, or a view from a mountaintop, these experiences inspire and transport us out of our everyday routines. Nature in its purest form will always lift our spirits. Panoramic vistas that stretch out before our eyes evoke a sense of expansion and possibility. They uplift our spirits, when in contrast, we may be experiencing compression, stress and exhaustion. It is no wonder our ancestors explored not only our natural world but the heavens above, as well. Just look up at the night sky when you are feeling like the world is caving in on you.

Our modern life complete with urbanization offers many conveniences, however we are far more removed from the great outdoors than ever before. In health studies, the disconnection between people and nature has a direct effect on mental health and mood disorders. Research indicates that access to nature, green spaces, and wide-open vistas improves overall well-being, and lowers levels of anxiety, stress and depression. The act of listening to birds in their natural habitats has been proven to contribute to greater attention, focus, and stress recovery. Exposure to natural spaces calms our frenetic lifestyles. A study in the Proceedings of the National Academy of Sciences (PNAS) in 2019 suggests that access to green spaces, particularly in childhood, provides mental health benefits and possibly lowers the risk of psychiatric disorders.[6] Spending time in nature is definitely good for our health and mental well-being.

Mother Nature's extraordinary, diverse display provides examples of perfect balance, harmony and order. These are the underlying guiding principles of all life and we greatly benefit by emulating her design. Mother Nature flourishes when her ecosystems are in balance. So it is with the human spirit. When things go out of whack and imbalances occur, we can experience extremes that are detrimental, like a flood of emotion or a drought of our very lifeforce. But through observation of the natural world, we understand that balance, harmony and order can be restored even when we face the most extreme conditions. Mother Nature constantly demonstrates her resiliency and ability to recover from external forces. For example, when a wildfire occurs and everything in its path is decimated, healing inevitably

6 Proceedings of the National Academy of Sciences (PNAS) in 2019: reference:https://www.pnas.org/content/116/11/5188

takes place and balance returns. From the ashes, new growth arises in the nutrient rich soil occurring in the aftermath of the fire. We too are resilient and able to restore ourselves from the adversity and trauma we may experience provided the conditions are right.

Being in nature allows us to experience everything more intensely and mindfully. It is immensely enjoyable to be outdoors and it makes most people feel better and lighter. While we are absorbing vital sunshine that provides essential vitamin D, we are also moving our bodies dynamically in concert with the rest of the natural world. When we wander, we are in motion, which gives us the sense that we are more alive. Wandering can be walking, hiking, kayaking, or sitting and observing at our own individual pace. It is also a metaphor for exploring life and opening ourselves up to new experiences. As we wander, we can step out of our own comfort zones and realize we have the potential to accomplish new things. This also is a powerful way to gain confidence and self-assurance.

After I turned 50, I experienced jumping out of a plane and soaring to the ground like a bird. The perspective from 13,000 feet above the earth was breathtaking. Three months later I swam with sharks off a coral reef near Bora Bora. Although I was certainly out of my comfort zone, being brave in the moment provided me with an extraordinary, rare moment that I otherwise would not have known. Both of these experiences were some of the most exhilarating and life affirming of my life and redefined what I thought was possible for myself.

We have accessibility to a myriad of places where we do not have to be encumbered by technology and distractions. By wandering, we can temporarily suspend our daily routines and worries. We can *walk out* a perplexing problem or shelf it altogether. For the past twenty years I have been walking in a nature preserve near my home. At least three times a week I walk my stress away by challenging myself with a steep ascent, focusing on wildlife such as birds, snakes, bugs, flowers, and the sound of ocean waves, as I keep moving towards peace and lightheartedness. Without a doubt, I always feel better and filled up when I return home.

There are both small and large ways to incorporate wandering into our daily routines. Sometimes all it takes is a few baby steps. If a person is homebound, opening the window might be the only way to access nature. Perhaps the first step is to literally step outside your door and notice your surroundings. Fresh air and sunshine can shift your physical and mental state in a matter of seconds. I often go outside after a long intense meeting or when I make an extended visit with a loved one in the hospital. The fresh air renews me and fills me up. If I have a busy day, I get myself out at lunchtime for a nature break of some sort.

If you have access to a garden or park, spend some time retreating there. There is great calmness instilled

by observing leaves blowing in the wind, or birds forag-
ing for insects. Any vibrant display of color in flowers,
foliage, or the array of clouds in the sky arouses our
senses. Sunrises and sunsets bring an ever changing,
awe-inspiring start and end to the day. Watching the
full moon rise is very grounding. Even a rainy day provides the meditative soothing sounds of droplets hitting
leaves or the ground. Nature moves in rhythms, cycles
and seasons, ebbs and flows. When we spend time
paying attention, we attune our own rhythms with the
collective life force moving through all living things.
Practice mindfulness and being fully present during
these moments.

MINDFULNESS EXERCISE

Try it right now. Wherever you are, spend just two minutes
taking in some piece of the natural world. Take deep,
calming breaths and feel connected to nature. Notice
the sky (blue, gray, cloudy, sunny, star filled?). What
sounds do you hear? (birds chirping, wind, train horns,
sirens, a lawnmower, dogs barking, waves crashing?)
What does your sense of smell evoke? (fresh cut grass,
mustiness, garden flowers, wet pavement, salty sea air?)
What can you reach out and touch in your surroundings?

(Stones or pavement beneath your feet, a tree trunk, rocks, a mossy facade?) What types of feelings does this experience evoke? Express gratitude for the present moment, wherever you are. Be grateful for the *here and the now.*

Beyond the patio and the garden are lakes, rivers, and the ocean, teeming with dynamic energy and of course life-giving water. Wandering on the beach allows you to absorb negative ions cast off by the crashing waves, as do pine tree needles in forests. That is why we innately feel so good in these places. Walking along a babbling brook is one of the most calming peaceful activities to experience. These activities open space and potential within us.

As we wander further from home, we have access to some of the most beautiful and awe- inspiring scenery in the world. Our forefathers had the far-sightedness to preserve our most breathtaking natural treasures for future generations. Thanks to them we can still explore these places in their pristine state. Our national parks offer a host of geological structure and form, natural habitats for wildlife, and a wide variety of flora and fauna. They also allow us to wander across thousands of miles of territory, on foot, bicycle, vehicle, or boat. Each park is diverse and unique. If you only get to one national park in your life, you will be better for the experience.

My husband and I intend to visit as many of them as possible. We are fortunate to live in proximity to many of them located in the Southwest. My favorite parks that we have visited to date are Zion, Bryce, and Joshua Tree. I find these parks, with their massive rock formations, to be both awe-inspiring and grounding. For me, the grounding element balances my hummingbird energy. If traveling to these parks in person is not an option for you, at least spend time wandering through them by way of the many documentaries available on television and online. The National Geographic channel has a series on each of the parks so that you can experience the points of interest virtually.

Beyond our borders there are many amazing places to explore and wander. Although I personally strongly favor natural environments, I also suggest exploring cities around the globe to take in the countless marvels of architecture, art, history, food and civilization. These sights are as life affirming as being in nature. The diversity of our global home enriches our lives and unifies us in our humanity. Beauty, art, and life flourish in every corner of our planet. Drink in as much as possible.

Over the years, I've noticed that I am drawn to wide open panoramas. I find these places evoke a sense of expansion. I first noticed this attraction years ago as I drove over the Cleveland Forest mountains and looked out to the desert surrounding Palm Springs below. This breathtaking view made me ask, why am I so moved by this experience? Again and again, I noticed that the more expansive the view, the freer and lighter I felt. There is something very peaceful and uplifting about looking out on the horizon in the distance. A few years ago I had the good fortune of spending twelve hours in Denali park in Alaska. As we drove for hours in search of bears and other wildlife, I was astonished by the vastness and openness of the park, with its sweeping landscape and glaciers rising in the distance. I have never seen so much open space. Later in that trip we took a small plane ride to the top of Mt. Denali and landed on a glacier. As we exited the plane to walk around for a little bit, I was unable to comprehend how small I was relative to the massive landscape around me. There were just six of us on that plane and we were the only life visible within a sweeping 360-degree view. I silently stood in awe pondering what a speck of life I am on this planet. I believe that wide open spaces are so soothing because they are the antithesis of our daily lives filled with schedules, obligations, and frenetic motion. These natural panoramas extend out and expand versus our typical feeling that everything else is coming at us. When you feel weighed down with worry or stress, head for the horizon.

As we have navigated through so many changes and uncontrollable circumstances forced upon us by the COVID-19 virus, for many of us the path has actually shifted. How we define ourselves may have changed. Some of us have lost our jobs, or businesses. The way we engage with the world has been drastically altered. Ahead lie new horizons that can bring change for the better, shaping and redefining how we live. Change forced upon us can speak to our higher nature as we evolve into a more flexible and adaptable version of ourselves. Where are these new horizons leading you?

WONDER ALWAYS

One of my favorite hiking buddies has as much wanderlust as I do. We often exchange our ideas for the next big trip. We have joked about starting a travel company together to satisfy our mutual love of adventure. Whenever the two of us go on a hike, she always suggests we continue to see what is around the corner. Typically, this will extend our hikes by double the distance and time that we had planned. It is our sense of wonder and curiosity that compel us to explore what is around the next corner. On occasion, we have to backtrack because what awaits us is not what we expected. Often however, our curiosity is rewarded with an amazing vista, or a magical gift of nature.

Curiosity and awe are innate qualities of childhood. It's fun to watch a toddler explore the world at full throttle. They touch, scrutinize, and feel their way through everything they come in contact with. That childlike wonder tends to wane as we get older. Our interactions with the world become familiar and mundane. We are more apt to stay within our comfort zone. While staying in our lane is safe and predictable, it is not very enriching. There are certainly times when it's suitable to do what is familiar. However, if we want to keep growing, we need to continue to cultivate that sense of wonder, learning and exploring new things.

Developing a sense of wonder and curiosity is as easy as asking ourselves questions. The simplest question to ask is "Why?" The great thing about asking *why* is that it opens up the possibility of innovation and change. We begin to understand that certain things in our lives don't have to be the way they are, that hope and faith in a different outcome is possible. Another great question to ask is "Why not?" Asking *why not* encourages us to find possibilities and the hope that anything might be feasible. Both questions allow us to be open to other outcomes than what we may be experiencing. I have included a lot of questions to prompt curiosity in the field notes of Chapter Five. Curiosity pushes us towards greater knowledge and insight than we already possess.

I believe wonder and awe are the magical components of being open to all possibilities. When we cannot see what's ahead, we may feel that there's no hope on the horizon. When our circumstances feel like winter, we do not know all the goodness that is in store for us in the spring. In order to shift we have to trust in the unseen. When we have a sense of awe for the good things in our lives and feel gratitude, we are more open to accepting the miracles that are awaiting us. Doing this work lays the foundation for an inner transformation. The outer manifestation reflects the inner work.

When life gets to be too much, I begin to count my blessings. I turn away from what has been eating at me and retreat within. I keep a running list of the little things that I appreciate. It may go something like this:

Finally finding time and space for exploring my creativity

Getting comfortable with uncertainty

Freedom and flexibility

Some rest

Coffee

Wondering and wandering frequently go hand in hand. When we wander, we can watch an awe-inspiring sunset or hike through a beautiful landscape. We can marvel at the beauty and magnificence of Mother Nature. As we retreat from the heavy burdens we experience in life, wandering propels us on our journey both physically and metaphorically. We set out on a path and perhaps we will keep going until we see what is around the next corner. It just may be the best and most unexpected vista ever.

FIELD NOTES ON AWE

We all have a lot of things we dream of doing. What if there were no boundaries or limitations on what you could experience? The ideas are endless...

- Create a bucket list of places you would like to go
- Research and plan a trip for the future
- Read *The Bucket List: 1000 Adventures Big & Small* by Kath Stathers
- Find a park near your home and spend some time observing nature
- Eat your lunch outdoors
- Adjust your lifestyle so that you can explore 1-2 new places a week
- Plan a hike with friends, bring a picnic to enjoy along the way
- Get away from city lights and do some star gazing
- Walk everywhere you can
- Watch the National Parks series on the National Geographic channel
- Pick up a copy of National Geographic's book entitled *100 Parks, 5000 Ideas* which features national, state and city parks to visit across the US and Canada

- Plan a visit to one or more National Parks
- Go camping with family or friends
- Instead of mindlessly surfing the web, research and plan some travel
- Plan a physical activity outside of your comfort zone
- Take lessons for a physical activity you would like to learn
- Hike in the forest
- Go bird watching
- Hike a portion of the Pacific Crest or Appalachian trail
- Join a group that partakes in active outdoor activities. REI has lots of activities for all levels
- Go to the beach and walk along the waves
- Wake up early to watch the sunrise
- Plant a garden
- Go whale watching
- Hire a guide to take you through a natural wonder
- See the northern lights
- Take a bike ride and explore your neighborhood and beyond
- Go fishing
- Take a road trip
- Learn rock climbing
- Visit a farm stand and buy some produce

- Take a Sunday drive and explore a new place
- Take a scenic drive (Route 66 / California's 17-mile drive/ Utah's Highway 24)
- Watch the sunset with a loved one
- Hike through fields of blooming wildflowers in the spring
- Take a hot air balloon ride
- Watch clouds float by on your back
- Swim in a coral reef
- Try falconeering
- Sleep in a yurt off the grid somewhere
- Kayak or canoe on a lake
- Snorkel in clear water by yourself
- Paddleboard
- Ski or snowboard during the winter
- Visit a dormant volcano
- Step outside for some fresh air during your workday
- Visit an animal sanctuary
- Keep going to see what is around the next corner

STEP AWAY

"Solitude is where I place my chaos to rest and awaken my inner peace."

—NIKKI ROE

"All journeys have secret destinations of which the traveler is unaware."

—MARTIN BUBER

What is a retreat? In its simplest form, it is the mindful intention to *come back to yourself.* When you are being pulled in many different directions by the demands and activities that command your attention, your pure source energy is fractalized and dispersed into the world. This energy, or light, is what we expend on the many things we do as we go about our days. Your inner light, potent and bright at its source, moves out towards the points of your attention, but rapidly dims as it moves further away from you, especially when circumstances require a high concentration of energy. As the light is continually cast outward, your inner reserves can be depleted if not consciously refilled. However, it is possible to maintain a reserve of this energy and keep it circulating in a balanced way. The process of energy circulation is the act of coming back to yourself to renew your lifeforce. There are many ways to refill the well including prayer, meditation and various rituals that I will share here. Retreating is coming full circle back to yourself, while stepping away from our outwardly expansive life — for a moment, a day, or longer. We learn to intentionally turn inward.

A wellness retreat is the epitome of stepping outside daily life to reconnect with yourself and perhaps a higher power. When most people think about going on a wellness retreat to restore their mind, body, and soul, they grapple with the cost, accessibility and challenge of carving out the time. Retreats are typically 3-7 days in length and carry a price tag of anywhere from $800 to $8000. In a perfect world, everyone would have access to these life-enhancing experiences. Imagine the impact of all of humanity intentionally focusing on their physical and mental health. I really believe that we are moving towards greater emphasis on integrative health and wellbeing and will shift towards more mindful experiences when everyone feels safe to resume travel in a post pandemic world.

Today, wellness retreats offer meditation, yoga, healthy eating or a combination of these and other practices. Typically, the cost includes accommodations, a series of programs and treatments, and your meals. Some retreats offer a full schedule of activities, while others focus on quiet, contemplative and reflective practices such as meditation. Silent retreats promote quietude and are rigorous in their own way. Regardless of the focus, the best retreats are located in awe-inspiring natural settings. The benefits can include exposure to different modalities of healing, body treatments, and self-development experiences. The downside is that you generally have to book them far in advance, which may or may not be convenient to your schedule. Life and current events can interfere with stepping away. In the spring of 2020 I, like many people, had to cancel travel plans due to the pandemic.

The focus of this chapter is to redefine what it means to retreat and to reframe stepping away so that it is accessible to anyone who desires to do so. Simply put, in the art of retreating, we have to be creative! It's imperative to take charge of our lives and foster the ability to create balance and wellness, even if we have to re-imagine what that looks like.

For me, retreating means finding a way to restore myself, with or without the help of others or an expensive program. A spectrum of possibilities exists depending on what is needed. Sometimes, all I am looking for is a place to find solitude to restore my inner peace. That may mean just a few moments *of* refuge amid whatever is going on around me. Occasionally I am in need of major downtime so escaping for a longer duration may be in order.

STEPPING AWAY FOR A MOMENT

Having a ritualistic cup of tea in solitude can be an immersive and restorative experience. In simple rituals like tea time we can be contemplative and inspired, or we can experience major shifts in mood and direction. Maybe doodling mindlessly is more your cup of tea. Whatever your inclination, when we practice stepping away through reclaimed moments, we begin to restore our source energy. Affectionately, I refer to these as adult timeouts.

Sometimes we just innately know when enough is enough, that we need a timeout to alter or shift a spiraling situation. Some of the go-to tactics I've utilized include lying on my closet floor in the dark for 15-20 minutes; taking a drive to nowhere in particular; locking the bathroom door (with a "do not disturb" sign) and making myself unavailable. When dealing with an emotionally charged issue such as a conflict with one of my children, receiving bad news, or arguing with my spouse, stepping away momentarily usually diffuses some of the emotion so that I do not overreact (and by the way, there are plenty of times when I didn't step away and I did overreact, ...I'm just saying). These little timeouts are powerful and effective ways of cord cutting that give me control over how I respond to the situation at hand. It's easier to step away and bite your tongue than to make amends for something that you regret saying in a heated moment. When I was working full time in the corporate world and had young children at home, I also employed this tactic for transitioning from the stresses of my workday to be fully present for my husband and kids. This simple act of closing the door to my bedroom and changing my clothes was all I needed to shift gears and turn towards my family and their needs after a busy day.

Another way in which I still use this momentary retreat is when I am dealing with crisis or bad news regarding a loved one. There are countless times when I have stepped away in a hospital, after a phone call, or during a face-to-face conversation with someone who has just received devastating news. I am notorious for holding space for the people in my life so that they have a safe, non-judgmental place to cry, rant, commiserate, or let a harsh reality seep in. It's my nature as a caregiver to be supportive. The goal as an empathic person however is not to take on another person's trauma and to feel as badly as they do. After holding space for someone going through trauma, it's incredibly important to check in with our own energy and make sure we aren't absorbing our loved one's pain, thereby compounding the problem. This is imperative in crisis situations and emotional, highly charged circumstances. Think about all of the front line caregivers that have been traumatized by the effects of the pandemic and what they are carrying on their minds and hearts, not to mention the physical toll. We need the space to release this stuff, which can be toxic if we hold onto it.

RETREAT FOR A DAY

Retreating for one day is much more doable than planning a 3-7 day getaway. Sometimes we only need a day to find some perspective and restore ourselves. This is also a cost-effective way to focus on your wellbeing without breaking the bank. There are numerous ways to plan a day-long retreat, and it does take a bit of planning. You cannot retreat with a toddler in tow or a houseful of kids. If you have young children, you will need to hire a babysitter or ensure the kids can spend the day with friends or family. If you are a caregiver yourself, you will need to make arrangements for someone to fill in for you. This might require hiring someone to be with an elderly parent or sick family member. The main goal is to clear your schedule of all obligations for a specific period of time (and fiercely stick with the plan). For example, if you are planning to retreat at home, you don't want to be catching up on housework like laundry or cleaning up dishes because you have the house to yourself. Another non-negotiable is distractions such as technology, and in particular, your phone.

Below I've outlined the daily retreat rituals that have worked for me over the years. You can find additional details in the field notes:

Create a Home Retreat (Most cost effective and relevant during stay at home restrictions)

The focus of the home retreat is to create a practice of compassionate care around yourself with a loosely formalized program that sets the intention to care for your body, quiet your mind and see your present life circumstances with clarity. Start by clearing your schedule, finding guided meditation videos or recordings, stocking your kitchen with healthy food you will prepare, and ensuring you have clean towels, cozy clothes, candles and other spa-like accessories that make you feel pampered and special. If you are a practitioner of meditation and other self-care rituals, this may be easy for you to envision. If you are a beginner, check out the resources in the field notes to help you get started.

Schedule your retreat for a half or a full day, incorporating elements of mindfulness, silence, reflection, spa treatments, healthy eating and rest. Lighting candles and other soothing enhancements such as essential oils and calming music can set the tone for a calm environment. You do not have to spend a lot of money to treat yourself. Set your intentions for the day, put your phone on *do not disturb* (allow for a few short breaks to check for *critical* communications only if absolutely necessary). Retreating means stepping away from the world. Communicate with co-workers and your boss in advance that you are unavailable for the day.

During your retreat, refrain from answering phone calls and emails. You may incorporate some inspirational videos, but refrain from all social media, as well as television. This is time for going within and refilling the well. Incorporate some light yoga poses and some form of hydrotherapy. Experiment with guided meditation or breathing techniques, eat some healthy food that you lovingly prepare, and take a nap if you desire. If you have access to the outdoors, spend some contemplative time in nature journaling or go for a walk. Cultivate an awareness of how you are feeling during the time you devote to yourself and be at peace with whatever may come up. Accept what is, and write out a list of intentions you want to take into your future after your day is complete.

One Day Spa Getaway

Many hotels and spas offer one day passes to their facilities. Living in southern California, I've come across a multitude of spas offering various amenities and price points. Research day spas in your area, close to home, so that you don't have to spend precious time traveling. Typically, you will pay a fee for the facility and an additional amount for any treatments you schedule. Retreating to a day spa in solitude or with a friend is a great way to get the benefits of a retreat in a short amount of time. One day retreats pack a power punch and deliver a big bang for the buck. While I love to get together with a girlfriend or my daughter for a day at the spa, I prefer to go in solitude and focus on self-care when I have the opportunity. You can schedule one or more treatments, enjoy the facilities such as the pool, spa, sauna and steam room and have a light meal. I will always schedule some body work such as massage or cranial sacral therapy since I carry a great deal of tension and emotion in my body. Some spas offer other services such as yoga, meditation, and other movement classes, depending upon their size and location. I once attended a one-day spa that had a demonstration kitchen and included a cooking class in the price. We were able to enjoy freshly made food from the garden on the property. In addition to a healthy meal, we were able to try cleansing tonics and beverages, and sample beauty products in the spa boutique all at a reasonable price. Often this type of getaway is all that's needed to feel whole again and get the needed break from our daily responsibilities.

Seasonal Retreat for a Day

Twice a year, on the winter and summer solstice, I give myself the entire day to reflect on the past six months, to recalibrate, and to set intentions for the coming six months. I've found it very beneficial to do this seasonally because these two parts of the year demand different aspects of me. The four seasons require our attention in different ways, whether it's planning for the holidays, the school year, summer break or the busyness of spring. Like many people, I am fairly depleted by the end of the year as a result of the pace and overindulgences of the holidays. I yearn to realign with my goals of health, balance and wellbeing. Summer typically is lighter and freer, but I do want to stay on track with my goals so I don't find myself drastically off course when life gets busier again in the fall.

There is something magical and powerful that occurs when you set your intentions on the auspicious days of the solstices, the shortest and longest days of the year. For one thing, if you plan for these two days every year, you are more committed to actually do this reflective work. Putting these dates on your calendar well in advance annually, ensures you are less inclined to schedule something else on these dates. The winter solstice celebrates the longest hours of darkness for the year, or the rebirth of the sun and symbolically holds a powerful energy for regeneration, renewal and self-reflection. I find the winter solstice reflection is more powerful than the tradition of making resolutions on New Year's day. The summer solstice marks the beginning of the season that contains the utmost bounty and beauty. It is also my favorite season of the year. My intentions and goals during this time reflect a lightness and optimism focused on creating more abundance, creativity and joy for myself and others. The goals during this season are blissful and nurturing.

During these two days each year, I hide away at a hotel or day spa and will begin with a treatment (usually some sort of bodywork). Afterwards, I spend time sitting by the pool if the weather is nice, or by the fireplace if it's cold or rainy, and reflect on my goals for the prior six months. I make an honest assessment of where my behavior and actions are in alignment with my goals, and where I need to refocus my attention. I will lovingly let go of what I did not achieve (as well as review what uncontrollable circumstances impacted my plans). I will treat myself to a wonderful lunch and a glass of champagne toasting my accomplishments. I will write out those things I would like to manifest for the coming six months and beyond.

Of course, the year 2020 was unlike any other. I found myself challenged by goal setting and intentions in the wake of so much uncertainty. We canceled a family vacation, my client work went away (as well as my income), other travel plans evaporated, and the activities that took their place were unchartered territory, such as reassuring my adult children that they were going to be okay in the midst of everything, working at the food bank and Salvation Army to support families in need, and trying to keep myself balanced, mentally in check, and fit through virtual yoga, connecting with friends and family, and trying to stay productively busy.

When the summer solstice rolled around on June 20th, all day spas remained closed due to the shutdown. For the first time in a very long time, I did not have a clue as to what goals I wanted to cultivate for the summer. My calendar pages remained empty. No travel plans, no real social activities, should I find new clients? Should I find a *real* job? I was faced with a new challenge as to how to plan for the future with no clarity of a timeline or an understanding as to how things might change. I shuffled my priorities. I find peace in the fact that I am not alone in navigating through this new reality. We are collectively figuring this out and sharing our wisdom and advice with each other in ways that are comforting. It's difficult and challenging to take things day by day. We do not know what's around the corner.

Today, it's about learning to be comfortable and flexible with whatever may come. I did not expect to be writing this book because I am always too busy to write. However, I managed to leverage the free time to write rather than be idle. I've always hoped to write a book but just wasn't sure how I might make it happen. The subject of retreating and taking care of ourselves seems very timely in the face of what we are presently enduring. For me, the underpinnings of this work have always been there, and now I have a reason to share my insight with others.

I did not accomplish the goals I set out to do in 2020, but the work I am doing is still on track with who I aspire to be. This year like any other is still about resilience, supporting and nurturing my loved ones, and being of value and service to the world in whatever ways I can. The outcomes may be wrapped in different packaging, but they remain in sync with my heart. I think it's important to keep an open dialogue about what we are feeling for the sake of our mental health and sanity. Trying to navigate the unknown is daunting, especially when our income stream is disrupted or the health of a loved one is in jeopardy. Making decisions for the well-being of an elderly parent or a spouse is challenging and stressful. Facing a health crisis or relationship crisis can bring us to our knees. Each of these experiences is scary on its own merit, let alone navigating a pandemic as well. The uncertainty is compounded, and we question whether or not we will emerge intact on the other side. The inner strength to endure, perhaps untapped, is like a reservoir within us. It's our personal responsibility to find it and connect with that part of ourselves. We are resilient and we will get through this.

A seasonal retreat can be whenever you choose. If you are celebrating the New Year and setting resolutions, you are already ritualistically on your way to retreating. This is an auspicious time to reflect on your life, say farewell to the old, and ring in the new. Other powerful times to do a seasonal retreat is in conjunction with a milestone birthday, before the birth of a baby, or after a divorce or death. These are the seasons of our lives so why not take time out to reflect on what these experiences mean to us and be inspired by what the next season will offer and require of us.

A Weekend Getaway

While a single day of getting away can do wonders, an optimal period of time to get away and feel the positive effects is a weekend. The nice thing about taking a weekend (roughly two and a half days) is that you're missing only a few hours of work, it's more likely you'll find someone to watch your children, and you can be back in time for dinner Sunday evening and be ready to step into the coming week without total upheaval.

Fifty-four hours is roughly the number of hours between Friday midday and Sunday evening. If at all possible, try to find a local experience that does not require many hours travel, which can be stressful. The goal is to be in a relaxed state for as long as possible. With a bit of planning and research, there are a number of ways to experience a local weekend retreat.

Many cities offer theme related retreats. These include yoga, meditation, nature, religious or spiritual, activities such as hiking, backpacking, as well as other special interests such as cooking, astronomy, or even UFO's (I kid you not). A great way to resource these events is through city guides, yoga studios, churches and out-door fitness clubs. There are a myriad of wellness centers that provide their own retreats and immersive learning experiences. These retreats offer specific self-growth op-portunities and programs in beautiful locations. Healing retreats can focus on specific challenges and issues that one might be facing.

A number of local boutique hotels and centers in southern California offer the environment for you to create your own organic retreat just as you would at home. These are peaceful, sustainable and inspired locations that offer a backdrop for your own practices, including mindful eating, yoga and meditation. As wellness becomes a popular focus of travel, more and more venues like this are popping up around the country. Search online for boutique hotels and wellness centers in your geographic region. And be sure to get any recommendations from friends and family.

While it is still an emerging practice in other parts of the country, southern California is home to some of the top sound bath centers in the nation. These are peaceful places to immerse yourself in an aural experience for deep relaxation and rejuvenation. The city of Joshua Tree, in the high desert north of Palm Springs, offers visitors the opportunity to explore the Integratron Sound Bath Dome and the national park on the same day. Once you begin to explore, you may be surprised to learn what you find in your own backyard! For inspiration, there are some ideas and resources in the field notes of this chapter.

To plan a budget conscious retreat, check out offerings through churches and other nonprofit organizations that are often set in summer camps and conference sites.

These locations may offer modest accommodations, but still provide a beautiful natural setting and the ability to get away and focus on self-reflection. Depending on the location, you may find yourself exploring the local area. Perhaps you will stumble upon an animal sanctuary, a local beekeeper or an artisan that you were not aware of. Absorbing a new community can spark the imagination and set you on a new path. These experiences add depth and color to our lives.

An Immersion Retreat

If you have the opportunity in your lifetime to experience an immersive retreat lasting seven to ten days, I highly recommend it. A seven-day retreat (or longer) requires both time and money, but can deliver a highly rewarding return on investment. An immersion retreat can be focused on a single theme such as yoga, meditation, wellness, or it can combine several practices. The criteria for selecting a retreat is highly personal and depends on your needs and interests. For some, a week-long meditation retreat might seem like torture while for others, it may be perfect. Before you commit to a specific retreat, make sure you do your homework and understand clearly what is being offered. For example, some retreats require you to share accommodations with another guest. If you like your personal space, it may not be a good fit for you.

A well established retreat center will have a sample daily itinerary for you to review before you book. Clarify what is and is not included in your stay so that there are no surprises or unexpected expenses. I highly encourage you to schedule a call with the program director at the retreat center to ask any questions you may have. They may also volunteer helpful information that is not available on their website. Equally important is understanding the refund policy in the event something unforeseeable comes up, particularly if a further investment in travel is required.

If you are attending a retreat in another country, additional travel to and from the location may be required. Understand what specific documents and other necessities are required in advance so that you are prepared. I was recently in charge of operations for a retreat in Joshua Tree, California, where participants attended from across the country and internationally as well. Many people ran into travel issues with flight connections and travel delays that caused logistical issues, causing some people to miss half of the retreat. This is so unfortunate when time is precious, and the registration fees are costly. Always plan your travel with plenty of time for inevitable travel snafus and delays. Understand what to bring for the weather and environment where you will be going. I strongly suggest asking the program director for a packing list. Travel as lightly as possible but be prepared for any weather. Layering of lightweight comfortable clothes gives you flexibility for temperature changes. Always bring a wind/rain proof coat. I travel with a light down jacket, even in the summer. I frequently wear it on the plane or use it as a pillow.

I prefer an immersion retreat that offers a variety of things to do and experience. An optimal program for me may include yoga, tai chi, meditation, bodywork, experiences in nature such as hiking, healthy food, massage, and a series of self-development programs, or a singularly focused program on a specific subject of interest. Equally important for me is *downtime* for self-reflection, unstructured exploration, and resting. If the itinerary is too full, it may feel like a marathon rather than a retreat.

Though it can be expensive, attending an immersion retreat can do wonders for the soul. After a very difficult year of my life, I committed to a fourteen day experience. I had no idea how I would put my life on hold for that amount of time, but deep down I knew that I needed to do so. I had emptied the gas tank between my mom's terminal illness, six weeks of living away from home with my father, and one of my children going through a difficult time during adolescence. I was tired and numb and had nothing left to give. I stepped away from my life, putting everything else on hold, hoping that I could reorient myself, in the wake of mother's passing. I vowed to honor her by rekindling the joy and spirit with which she lived her life. I decided to make a trek to Italy with a close friend and visit Tuscany and take a pilgrimage to Assisi, one of the cities that was on my mother's bucket list, but a place she did not make it to during her life. The first few days were a blur (I slept a lot and was disoriented by the time change). Slowly I felt myself coming back on line. My energy returned and I started to notice my surroundings...the beautiful vistas...the taste of food, the smell of the blooming trees in the courtyard where I stayed. I found my joy and laughter again. I ran through the hills of the countryside, I slept in, I ate a lot of pasta. I felt like I was experiencing my own version of EAT, PRAY, LOVE. I did not allow myself to feel guilty for stepping away from my family. I needed to take a break and be there for myself. I returned from that experience renewed. I still had a great deal of grief and parenting challenges to work through, but I reconnected with my inner strength and wisdom to empower me as a result of that experience. It was the best decision I could have made for my well-being and my sanity.

With so many different options for retreating, there really is no excuse not to step away from your life when the need arises. If you find yourself in need of a moment, take the moment. When necessary, put yourself in timeout. Listen to your inner guidance to discern what you need. Set the intention to give yourself a day of retreat. Maybe it's your birthday present to yourself. Celebrate your successes and all of the things that you have accomplished with your life. Reflect on where you have been and where you are going. Spend a day in solitude, setting your goals and establishing a roadmap for them. Get a massage and have a glass of champagne. Kick the family out of the house and have a spa day at home. Step it up a notch and check into a local boutique hotel for a night or weekend. Research and plan a weekend away. Explore what's just beyond your neighborhood. Step outside your comfort zone and try something new. Attend a local self-development weekend seminar. Try a yoga retreat or nature getaway. Explore sound healing. If the opportunity arises, plan an immersion retreat near home or far away. There are times in our life when we are in transition, depleted and in need of some nurturing and care. These are not luxuries. They are necessities. Take impeccable care of yourself, especially when you are in a fragile state. Step away from the madness, the chaos, the mundane, the unbearable, the toxic, the go-go-go and the do-do-do. Retreat.

FIELD NOTES FOR STEPPING AWAY

HOW TO CREATE A HOME RETREAT (ONLINE FREE RESOURCE):

https://www.tarabrach.com/create-home-retreat/#sampleschedule)

Determine your schedule and plan for a day and remove distractions (partner/children/work/obligations)

Gather items to make your sanctuary more enriching:

- Candles
- Yoga mat
- Soft blanket
- Journal
- Health food/beverages
- Bath products/essential oils
- Inspiring reading material
- Guided meditations (YouTube/Headspace/DailyOM)
- Other items that resonate with you

Plan a schedule for the day

Set your intentions

Incorporate elements from the Art of Retreating such as meditation/reflection/yoga/journaling/walking in nature/ hydrotherapy/preparing healthy meal/mindfully enjoying your meal/napping/music/art or creative activity

Accept what comes up

Focus on areas where you feel out of balance

Journal and write intentions for change

End in practice of gratitude

Read a mindfulness magazine for other ideas and variations. A few I like are:

- **Breathe:**
  https://www.breathemagazine.com
- **Organic Spa Magazine:**
  https://www.organicspamagazine.com
- **Yogajournal:**
  https://www.yogajournal.com

Online Resource for World's Largest Collection of Authentic Wellness Retreats: https://retreat.guru

MEDITATION RETREATS

- **Ananda in the Himalayas** — Uttaranchal, India
  https://www.anandaspa.com/en/home
- **Green Gulch Farm Zen Center** — Muir Beach, CA
  https://www.sfzc.org/practice-centers/green-gulch-farm
- **Insight Meditation Society** — Barre, Massachusetts
  https://www.dharma.org
- **Holy Isle of Arran** — Isle of Arran, Scotland
  https://www.holyisle.org
- **Miraval** — Tucson, Arizona and Austin, Texas
  https://www.miravalresorts.com
- **Muktawan 7 Day Meditation Retreat** — Phuket, Thailand
  https://meditationforyourself.wordpress.com/2015/04/28/muktawan-retreat/
- **Osho Meditation Resort** — Pune, India
  https://www.osho.com/osho-meditation-resort
- **Rolling Meadows Meditation Retreats** — Tulum, Mexico
  https://rollingmeadowsretreat.com
- **Simple Peace** — Assisi, Italy
  https://www.assisiretreats.org
- **Shambhala Mountain Center** — Red Feather Lakes, Colorado
  https://www.shambhalamountain.org
- **Stillpoint Lodge** — Halibut Cove, Alaska
  https://stillpointlodge.com

- **The Raj Ayurveda Health Spa** — Fairfield, Iowa
https://theraj.com
- **Travaasa** — Maui, Hawaii and Austin, Texas
https://travaasa.com/hana/

YOGA RETREATS

- **Anamaya Resort**, Costa Rica
https://anamaya.com
- **Ananda Spa**, India
https://www.anandaspa.com/en/home
- **Bali Spirit Festival**, Bali
https://www.balispiritfestival.com
- **Blue Osa**, Costa Rica
https://www.blueosa.com/about-us/
- **Civana Wellness Resort and Spa**
https://civanacarefree.com
- **Omega Institute**, New York
https://www.eomega.org
- **Phool Chatti Ashram**, India
https://www.phoolchattiyoga.com
- **Santosha Yoga Retreat**, British Columbia
https://santosha-yoga-retreats.com
- **Skylagoon**, Iceland
https://www.skylagoon.com
- **Suncokret Retreats**, Croatia
https://www.suncokretdream.net

- **The Sanctuary**, Thailand
  https://www.thesanctuarythailand.com
- **Zuna Yoga Teacher Training**, Bali
  https://www.zunayoga.com

WELLNESS INSTITUTES

- **Center for Health and Wellbeing**
  https://yourhealthandwellbeing.org
- **Chopra Center**
  https://chopra.com
- **Civana Wellness Resort and Spa**
  https://civanacarefree.com
- **Esalen Institute** — Big Sur, California
  https://www.esalen.org
- **Global Wellness Institute**
  http://globalwellnessinstitute.org
- **Kripalu Center for Yoga and Health**
  https://kripalu.org
- **Maharishi International University**
  https://www.miu.edu
- **National Wellness Institute**
  https://nationalwellness.org
- **Omega Institute**
  https://www.eomega.org
- **Smith Center for Healing and the Arts**
  https://smithcenter.org

- **The Well**
  https://www.the-well.com
- **UCLA Mindful Awareness Research Center (MARC)**
  https://www.uclahealth.org/marc/
- **1440 Multiversity**
  https://www.1440.org

INTEGRATIVE HEALTH CENTERS

List of Integrative Health Centers in every state:

- **Resource:**
  https://www.researchforwellness.com/health-centers
- **Optimum Health Institute**:
  http://www.optimumhealth.org

WELLNESS RETREATS

- **Canyon Ranch Spa**
  https://www.canyonranch.com
- **Diamond Lodge**, Belize
  https://www.diamondlodgebelize.com
- **Journey to Sacred Iceland**
  https://www.madeleinemarentette.com/journey-to-sacred-iceland-trip

- **Le Monaste`re des Augustines**, Quebec City
  https://monastere.ca/en
- **Pritkin Longevity Center and Spa** — Miami, Florida
  https://www.pritikin.com
- **Skyterra Wellness Retreat** — North Carolina
  https://skyterrawellness.com
- **Velas Resorts** — Puerto Vallarta, Mexico
  https://www.velasresorts.com/spas

WELLNESS FOCUSED TRAVEL AGENCIES

- https://www.fountain-of-you.com
- https://www.journeysthatfit.com
- https://lotustrips.com
- https://www.mytripwell.com
- http://souljournadventure.com
- https://www.suitedreamstravel.net
- https://vacayou.com
- https://www.vipwellnessgetaways.com
- https://www.wellnesstourismassociation.org

That should get you started. If you want some assistance in your planning, go to the Art of Retreating website at:

https://www.artofretreating.com

10

FLOW

"And I said to my body softly... 'I want to be your friend.' It took a long breath and replied... 'I have been waiting my whole life for this.'"
—NAYYIRAH WAHEED

PARTY SHOULDER

During my senior year of college, I experienced a debilitating migraine for the first time in my life. It was right before exams in financial management, statistics, and advanced calculus. I barely made it through my exams and it reflected in my test grades. Apparently, this was a stress induced event.

While preparing to host a fundraiser for a charity my young daughter supported, I tweaked my back. My torso was contorted into the shape of an S and my spine was in complete spasm. This was the result of overdo-ing, as I did not accept any of the generous offers of assistance.

In the past ten years, while hosting a variety of events, I have experienced significant pain shooting up and down my right arm. In some cases, the pain was so intense I could not lift my arm at all. For the guests, these events went off seamlessly, but for me, the physical suffering was profound. Eventually I endearingly named this syndrome, *"party shoulder."* I am now fully aware of the self-induced consequences I will face whenever I don't exercise restraint and take the time for proper rest, which will result in a case of party shoulder. It is the cumulative effect of putting too much on my plate. These days, it is my intention to refrain from party shoul-der, at all costs. Our bodies are our closest confidants and want to assist us in staying in a state of flow and alignment. They literally and figuratively always signal to us when we are out of alignment. We need to befriend our bodies and listen to what they are telling us before we do real damage.

FLOW

The simple definition of flow is the action of moving in a steady, continuous stream without obstructions. In positive psychology, flow is referred to as a state of being in the zone where a person performing some activity is fully immersed in a feeling of energized focus, full engagement, and enjoyment in the process of the activity.[7] In both states, flow is energy moving. As with water, energy must move or it will stagnate. When there are obstacles or impediments in a stream or a river, the water either finds a way to bypass these objects or it builds up, ceases to move, and creates toxic imbalances.

Take a moment to marvel at the beautiful design of the human body. The body's systems are microcosms of miracles fueled by life force and rhythms. These systems are in a perpetual state of flow and comprise the framework that carries us through life. Our bodies dynamically express themselves as strong, rigorous, flexible, adaptive, enduring and reliable vehicles. Without conscious prompting, life force pulsates throughout our body. Our hearts beat and push blood through our circulatory systems. Our brains process a multitude of instructions like supercomputers, and all of our other bodily systems go about their business with little, if any, conscious input from us.

7 https://en.wikipedia.org/wiki/Flow_(psychology)

Our individual responsibility in managing the wellness of our body systems is maintaining a reasonable level of balance, nutrition, hydration, rest, exercise, and stress management. The body is incredibly resilient and, for the most part, can handle a wide range of tolerances and retain stability. Each of the microcosmic systems flow flawlessly unless impeded by inside or outside forces. How advantageous this is for us as we confront various challenges and rigors to maintain balance in all the different areas of our lives. Yet, we almost take for granted the autopilot characteristic of our bodies until we find ourselves out of alignment.

Inevitably our life conditions fluctuate and demand different levels of energy at different times. During challenging periods, our bodies may experience imbalances such as lack of sleep and rest, nutritional deficiencies, dehydration, overindulgence, allergies, illnesses, and stress responses such as anxiety. Fortunately, these situations are typically temporary and our bodies are capable of auto correcting back to a state of homeostasis.

Other times, we may experience imbalances that last for a longer duration, or even an entire season of our life. During extended periods of endurance, the immune system may be compromised and compound the effects of physical neglect. Secondary implications including illness, disease, and mental health issues such as mood disorders may arise from prolonged imbalances. Sleep deprivation can exacerbate any of these conditions. Unresolved trauma can be debilitating and may create health issues down the road. Unresolved trauma is stuck energy. Fortunately, these scenarios can be reversed with proper care and attention, if acknowledged before more chronic issues develop.

The practice of retreating can alleviate many imbalances through modification of behaviors that are not in alignment with our natural state of health and wellness. Let's face it, each of us will experience being out of alignment many times throughout our lives. Circumstances can turn on a dime, creating all sorts of upheaval. No one can keep it all together at all times. Each of us is doing the best that we can, but we greatly benefit from developing an active awareness to acknowledge when life is not flowing optimally. The habits discussed in this field guide provide avenues for identifying misalignments and imbalances in order to correct them.

Going with the flow indicates an abdication of resistance and accepting a situation that we are experiencing rather than forcefully trying to control or alter it. When we face a challenging situation in our life, we are inclined to want to fix things, or alternatively run away from the problem so that we can avoid pain. Consciously or unconsciously, we create the obstacles and impediments to our flow when we resist or ignore the challenges and trauma in our lives. Pain and other difficult emotions must flow through us, or they will create stagnation and lead to more serious issues. What is that pain trying to teach us about ourselves? Unexpressed emotional issues build up in the body and physically impact us by showing up as physical and emotional pain, blockages and even disease. Various methodologies are effective for releasing emotion, stress, and trauma from our physical bodies and our minds. I refer to these modalities as *body tune ups.*

Body tune ups are essential to our well-being because in addition to the weight of our bodies, we carry a great deal of emotion, toxins, and difficult experiences within our framework, which sometimes feels like the weight of the world. If you are an empath, as I am, you may carry the weight of other people's experiences, as well. This is why you must consciously create compassionate boundaries for yourself and clear the energy of your own field on a regular basis.

In addition to self-reflection, slowing down, nourishment, awe, and stepping away, body tune ups are a powerful tool for optimizing our wellbeing. Body tune ups include movement and exercise, bodywork such as massage, various integrative practices, and care of the physical self. While I am only touching on a few of the effective modalities that have worked for me and those in my circle, there are many more. These are complementary modalities to other healing practices such as counseling, therapy, and mainstream treatments that may be recommended by your doctor. Body tune ups are not a substitute, but an enhancement to a fully holistic plan for your overall wellness. Always seek the professional advice of a practitioner of your choosing and consult with them about incorporating any of the practices mentioned here.

BODYWORK

"Sometimes you don't feel the weight of something you've been carrying until you feel the weight of its release."
—POWEROFPOSITIVITY.COM

Some people think that bodywork, such as massage, is a luxury. However, research reveals many advantages to having regular body tune ups. The various forms of bodywork, including massage, can be seen as part of a preventative health regimen by lowering the rate of injury, increasing flexibility, as well as providing mental health benefits. During bodywork, you are in a passive state by allowing others to do the work for you. This creates the space to rest, relax, and reset the mind. Body tune ups are rejuvenating because they allow for your autonomic nervous system to release and recalibrate. Bodywork is a ritual of self love by consciously and intentionally giving time and space to yourself. Below are some of the more effective practices that I have utilized on their own or in combination for tuning up my own body.

Massage

The most widely known conventional and sought after form of bodywork is massage because of the known benefits to mind, body and spirit. There are many different variations of therapeutic massage (see field notes) that enhance the body's restorative function and flexibility. Typically a trained therapist will engage in light to medium touch to relieve tension, relax the body and increase blood circulation. Most individuals feel a sense of calm and relaxation after a massage. Deep tissue massage can be used to effectively address chronic issues, areas of injury, and relief from anxiety and tension. When seeking out a massage therapist, do your research and experiment with different modalities to see what your body responds to best. Make sure the massage therapist is a licensed practitioner, has a depth of experience and is affiliated with a reputable organization.

Cranial Sacral Therapy

Cranial sacral therapy (CST) is the manipulation of the skull and sacrum through a series of light holds by the practitioner. The movements are subtle and sometimes barely detectable, yet I am amazed that I continue to feel the positive effects well after the session, as I do with regular massage.

By lightly holding various areas of the body, typically around the head and the spinal cord, the body is able to self correct and alleviate ailments such as chronic pain, injuries, tension, anxiety and neurological impairment. The benefits include relief of compression in the head, neck and back which, like many people, is where I hold my tension. Gentle manipulation affects the flow of the cerebrospinal fluid between the head and the base of the spine, which nourishes the brain and spinal cord. CST uses a light touch to examine membranes and movement of fluids in and around the central nervous system promoting a feeling of wellness and boosting health and immunity.[8]

Although CST is considered a subset of therapeutic massage, I find it more essential because it has been so beneficial in my own healing. I compare my experience with cranial sacral therapy as *decompression* on a grand level. During my sessions, I can actually feel my brain

8 Cranial Sacral Therapy benefits, Cleveland Clinic https://www. my.clevelandclinic.org/heath/treatments/17677-cranialsacral-therapy

expanding and the circulation of fluids in my head, which my therapist refers to as *ooey gooey*. The sensations that I experience are very similar to how I feel when I see wide panoramic vistas and horizons. The feeling CST evokes is spaciousness within. I also feel keenly alert after a session. I am consciously more aware of fine details and color. Because CST manipulation is so gentle, it is a fantastic modality of treatment for individuals of all ages. I've listed some of the common ailments and disorders that CST can improve in the field notes of this chapter.

Acupuncture

Emanating from ancient traditional Chinese medicine, acupuncture is an effective healing modality for a variety of issues both physical and mental. Acupuncture works in conjunction with the *Qi* (pronounced 'chee') which is also known as our life force. Traditional practitioners work with over two thousand points on the human body which are connected by meridians. Inserting ultra thin needles at various meridian points, the Qi is activated to flow freely, which improves health conditions.

The needles cause minimal or no discomfort if placed correctly during a treatment. Depending upon the ailment being addressed, acupuncture can create either a relaxed or energized state. In addition to acupuncture, techniques such as friction, suction, and acupressure may be applied during different treatments. Like CST, acupuncture is believed to stimulate the central nervous system and activate the body's natural healing abilities via the muscles, the brain and the spinal cord. It may not be for everyone, and I recommend consulting with your doctor to ensure it is a safe and complementary treatment for your overall health and wellness.

As with massage practitioners, it is imperative to find a licensed acupuncturist who has proper training and credentials.

A sampling of health issues that may be effectively treated with acupuncture are listed in the field notes.

Rolfing

Rolfing is another form of soft tissue manipulation similar to therapeutic massage that focuses on the structural integration and posture of the body. Rolfing was developed in 1920 by the pioneer Dr. Ida P. Rolf, Ph.D, during her research in biochemistry.[9] This form of bodywork is organized around the whole body in space and focuses on the manipulation of the myofascial system of connective tissue. Rolfing is a very holistic approach to healing the strain on the entire body resulting from

9 Rolfing, pioneer Dr. Ida Rolf. PhD http://www/rolf.org/rolfing.php

patterns developed in life. It focuses on more efficient use of muscles so creating an economical use of energy. The benefits of rolfing include reducing chronic stress, enhancing neurological function and improved flexibility and rehabilitating injuries. Unlike massage, rolfing is focused on improving body alignment and structural functioning. A rolfing practitioner will work on the entire body structure rather than specific areas of tension or injury. Rolfing requires multiple successive sessions to integrate the structural progression across the body. Typically, ten or more sessions may be necessary. Practitioners are trained at The Rolf Institute in Boulder, Colorado. Certification requires two years of study and continued education for six years. You can find a licensed practitioner in your area by contacting the Rolf Institute.[10]

Movement

It comes as no surprise that our bodies need to move for our overall health and wellness. We all know the value of exercise and maintaining a regular physical routine to stay vital, fit and healthy. Have you ever wondered at what point in time exercise became working out? You may be surprised to learn that the etymology of the expression dates back to 1922 meaning *strenuous*

10 Dr. Ida Rolf Institute http://www.rolf.org

physical exercise. I find it very interesting that when we exercise (through movement) we are *working something out.* At its roots, this expression seems complementary to my belief that movement and flow are one. Working out is the flow and release of energy that is necessary in the pursuit of vitality.

By today's definition, working out can be strenuous and intense. We put our bodies through the paces to build muscle and endurance, maintain cardiovascular fitness, retain muscle tone and look and feel our best. Men and women alike participate in bootcamps, do weight training, and engage in a variety of aerobic activities. I personally incorporate endurance activities such as climbing outdoor stairways, distance running and hiking.

The practices I would like to focus on here is subtle in nature and profoundly beneficial to our mind-body-spirit wellbeing. They are like energetic showers cleansing the emotional and physical blockages that result from stress. As with our diets, when we are under pressure, we may not be able to maintain our regular regimen of exercise and fitness. But lack of movement can actually compound and amplify the stress and anxiety we feel as the energy simply has no where to flow. The following practices, that I endorse, refill the well and keep our lifeforce pulsing through our bodies. These holistic practices are complementary to your regular fitness routine and can be enjoyed for the rest of

198 The Art of Retreating

your life because they are gentle movements that are easy on the body, help maintain flexibility, strength, and balance, and can be modified for any age or ability. You can also do them anywhere and anytime.

Yoga

Yoga is a universal form of movement that offers holistic benefits for the mind, body, and spirit. Various forms of secular and spiritual yoga are practiced around the world today by young and old alike. When I started yoga in the '90s, it was just beginning to take off in the United States and classes were few and far between. Today it is nearly impossible to walk down the street without seeing a person with a yoga mat tucked under their arm (in California, at any rate).

Yoga emerged as a philosophy over 5,000 years ago in ancient India. A session consists of a combination of set physical postures or *asanas*, breathing techniques and relaxation. Meditation may also be combined with some yoga practices.

Today there are many variations of yoga to experience. Hot yoga and core yoga are incredibly popular. These are more aligned with the rigorous forms of working out previously mentioned. As with any physical regimen, consult your health practitioner to ensure that yoga is a complementary practice for your overall health. New students should notify their instructors of injuries or health issues before beginning a session. If possible, enroll in a beginner's course that focuses on form and alignment as well as an introduction to basic poses and breathing.

The beautiful thing about yoga is that it is not a competitive sport. In fact, the basic tenet of yoga is that you come to yoga exactly where you are in life physically, mentally and spiritually. Competition and comparison to others is actually discouraged. In the field notes of this chapter, I have provided a list of different yoga practices you may want to explore. As with meditation, it is only through experience that we can determine what resonates with each of us. Many yoga studios offer different types of classes so I encourage you to see what works best for you. As a result of the pandemic, many yoga studios have closed or are only offering classes online. If there is a silver lining in this situation, the classes are now globally accessible to anyone. You can practice with a community right from your own home and all you really need is enough space for you and your yoga mat. Namaste.

Tai Chi

As with some of the other movement techniques, Tai Chi (pronounced 'tie-chee') originates from the East. It is actually a form of Chinese martial arts that is practiced for a variety of reasons, including defense training. Tai Chi is captivating to observe because of the graceful flow of movements that are rhythmically performed in a slow, focused manner. Perhaps you have seen a group of people practicing Tai Chi in a park. The movements flowing from one to another have a hypnotic meditative quality and are accompanied by deep breathing. The symbolism behind Tai Chi is that one must first be balanced internally in order to be balanced on one's feet. Steadiness comes from within. The health benefits of this gentle practice are significant, as cited in many prestigious journals. Harvard Medical School describes Tai Chi as *medication in motion*[11] and states there is growing evidence that this mind-body practice has value in treating or preventing many health problems as well as the rehabilitation of many conditions associated with age. The broader appeal of Tai Chi is that all age groups and abilities can participate in this remarkable form of movement. As with yoga, community Tai Chi groups can be found across the country through a bit of research. I was curious about this practice and researched the fundamentals on the internet. I taught myself the basic Tai Chi movements from watching a YouTube video. I have included resources for Tai Chi instruction in the field notes.

[11] www.health.Harvard.edu/staying-healthy/the-health-benefits-of-tai-chi

Qigong

Qigong (pronounced 'chee-guhng'), like Tai Chi, is another form of gentle exercise derived from the martial arts. While many of the movements may be similar to Tai Chi, there are subtle variations, including the philosophy that both internal and external movements take place simultaneously. The internal movements (flows) are referred to as *neigong* meaning 'internal power.' Qigong provides mental clarity through the alleviation of emotional stress. In China, Qigong is utilized to improve circulation, relieve pain and joint swelling and regulate balance of internal organs. For those that want to dive deeper, there is a more profound level of meaning to the movements of this practice which represent a total system of energy work and personal development, in alignment with Taoist traditions.

Many people practice Qigong daily in an outdoor setting blending the rhythms of the body with the sounds and rhythms of nature. The benefits of a daily practice are peace, calmness, and a healthier body. While Qigong is not as prevalent in the West, it is gaining traction with holistic, integrative health and wellness programs. To learn more, see the resources provided in the field notes.

Move Everyday

With ever increasing amounts of time sitting in front of computers, we are becoming the sedentary generation. Unfortunately, sitting has become the new smoking. An inactive lifestyle is quite harmful. Our bodies are designed to move and flow. That is how we work things out and maintain our flexibility, as well as other bodily systems. Movement in whatever form is beneficial to our mental and emotional state. When we tune up our body, we increase our vitality, reduce our stress, provide fresh oxygen to our cells, and improve our flexibility. When we are stagnant, we impede the flow of our energy and in turn, things start to break down. You don't have to be super athletic or even go to a gym to move your body. Start with a twenty minute walk in nature. Tackle some hills or a familiar trail near home. See if you can increase your heart rate even a bit. Put on some music and dance. Get on a bicycle and ride around the neighborhood. Take a yoga class or watch a video on Tai Chi or Qigong and follow along until the movements feel natural. Every step you take, every move you make, is activating the flow of the energy through your body and your mind. I promise you will feel better when you move every day.

Somatic Therapy

While touching upon various forms of body tune ups that provide healing in this chapter, I think it's important to mention the topic of somatic therapy. Somatic means *of or relating to the living body*. Somatic therapy is a form of psychotherapy that focuses on the mind-body connection typically dealing with forms of trauma, stress, anxiety, depression and grief. The healing process begins with the body and explores body tension, sensations, and gestures in conjunction with awareness, dialogue, touch and movement. The resulting counseling/therapy sessions lead to greater peace, comfort, and ease.

Somatic therapy can be transformative work, opening the door to abundant joy and freedom in life. The practice was developed by Dr. Peter Levine, PhD, based on the idea that trauma can lead to dysfunction of the nervous system through what is known as the *freeze response* where parts of the body tense up and stay that way long after the threat or experience disappears.[12] With mental health issues and human suffering on the rise, this form of therapy may be an alternate form of treatment which doesn't require prescription drugs with long-term side effects. As with all mental health issues and conditions, consult the recommendations of your doctor as a starting point for your overall care plan.

12 Dr. Peter A. Levine, PhD; https://www.somaticexperiencing.com

Go with the Flow

We understand that our minds and our bodies are woven together in a constant dance with one another, each greatly impacting the function of the other. Peace and calm derive from a state of resiliency that is a delicate balance of flexibility rather than rigidity, and flow rather than stagnation. Allow your body to move and be moved so that thoughts and emotions ebb and flow like the tide. Learn not to hold onto stressful experiences, trauma, drama and chaos. Let them go for your overall well-being. Each of us has our weak spots and, more likely than not, stress is going to manifest in our most vulnerable body parts. Whether it be party shoulder, a migraine, irritable bowel syndrome or a bad back, your body is giving you warning signs. Listen to what it is telling you and bring it back into alignment by releasing what does not serve you. Keep your body well tuned and go with the flow.

FIELD NOTES FOR BODY TUNE UPS AND FLOW

TYPES OF THERAPEUTIC MASSAGE[13]

Therapeutic Massage Techniques

- **Swedish Massage:** Flowing, kneading, and passive joint movement techniques. Promotes release of tensions and general relaxation. Stimulates nerve endings in the skin and connective tissue, increasing blood and lymph circulation.

- **Deep Tissue Massage**: Work done deep within the muscles and connective tissue. Slow strokes and deep finger pressure work to release contracted areas of muscles and surrounding tissue.

- **Reflexology:** Pressure point holds stimulate reflex channels. Effective for areas of tension or pain. Hands, feet, and ear pressure points are massaged to promote general well-being.

- **Neuromuscular Massage:** Advance massage techniques effectively treat chronic pain and injuries. Improves muscular and postural imbalances.

13 Johns Hopkins Medicine, https://www.hopkinsmedicine.org/integrative_medicine_digestive_center/services/therapeutic_massage.html

- **Craniosacral Therapy:** Light touch holds work within the natural flows of the body. Results in deep relaxation and encouragement of the body's alignment and natural healing ability.

- **Lymph Drainage Therapy:** Light pressure facilitates increased movement of lymph fluid. Complements treatment of auto-immune disorders, cancer treatments, surgery, and contributes to wellness through improved immune response.

- **Reiki:** Light touch, accesses Universal Life Energy. Can speed healing, reduce pain, and decrease symptoms.

- **Hot Stone Massage Therapy:** This 90 minute session uses a variety of large and small smooth heated stones to melt away tension and stress, resulting in deep relaxation.

CRANIAL SACRAL THERAPY

Common disorders that CST can help relieve:

- ADD/ADHD
- Anxiety and panic attacks
- Autism
- Brain and spinal cord trauma
- Central nervous system disorders
- Chronic neck and back pain
- Dyslexia

- Fascial pain
- Fibromyalgia and chronic fatigue
- Learning disabilities
- Migraines and headaches
- Motor-coordination impairment
- Post-traumatic stress disorder
- Scoliosis
- TMJ disorder

ACUPUNCTURE

Common conditions that Acupuncture can help relieve:

- Addiction
- Anxiety
- Back and neck pain
- Depression
- Digestive Issues
- Headaches and migraines
- Insomnia
- Menstrual pain
- Neurological disorders
- Respiratory
- Sciatica

THE SIX BRANCHES OF YOGA[14]

- **Hatha yoga** — the physical and mental branch designed to prime the body and mind
- **Raja yoga** — this branch is focused on meditation and structured adherence to a series of disciplinary steps called the eight limbs
- **Karma yoga** — The path of service that creates a future free of negativity and selfishness
- **Bhakti yoga** — The path of devotion and positive channeling of emotions to cultivate acceptance and tolerance
- **Jnana yoga** — The path of yoga related to wisdom, scholarly pursuits, and developing the intellect
- **Tantra yoga** — The path of ritual, ceremony, and consummation of relationships

TRADITIONAL TYPES OF YOGA

- **Ashtanga yoga** — A structured practice of yoga that follows a series of six established sequences of postures. This form of yoga follows the movement of the breath.
- **Bikram yoga** — Hot yoga practice in a heated room at a temperature of 100+ degrees. There are 26 poses done in sequence.

14 The six branches of yoga; reference https://www.medicalnewstoday.com

- **Hatha yoga** — A practice of yoga that focuses on physical postures and are conducted in a gentle manner

- **Iyengar yoga** — The incorporation of props such as blocks, straps, blankets and bolsters to focus on alignment.

- **Jivamukti (Vinyasa) yoga** — A spiritual form of yoga including yoga philosophy, chants, meditation and breathwork known as pranayama. Jivamukti is a Sanskrit word which means liberation while living.

- **Kripalu yoga** — A form of yoga in which the student looks inward to learn from oneself. This form of yoga includes asanas and a final relaxation pose called shavasana (corpse pose).

- **Kundalini yoga** — Kundalini is a form of energy yoga aimed at releasing pent up energy. As with vinyasa yoga, kundalini incorporates asanas, breathwork and meditation. Kundalini means *coiled like a snake* in Sanskrit.

- **Power yoga** — Today power yoga is widely practiced as a form of athletic yoga. Power yoga has its roots in traditional ashtanga yoga practice but is an amplified variation and may include elements of hot yoga as well.

- **Sivananda yoga** — An integrative form of lifestyle yoga which includes five elements: breathwork, relaxation, diet, exercise and positive thinking.

- **Viniyoga** — A form of yoga that is primed around anatomy and yoga therapy. This yoga may be practiced by those with physical limitations or injuries. Teachers require additional training in anatomical structure.

- **Yin** — This practice is very restorative and focuses on the release of tension in key joints of the body such as the shoulders, neck and hips. The poses are passive so that the body releases tension over time.

- **Prenatal yoga** — Postures are designed for pregnancy and the safety of the baby and the mother before birth.

- **Restorative yoga** — Like yin yoga, this practice is focused on relaxation. Unlike traditional yoga practices, there are only four to five poses incorporated during a session so that muscles release, promoting deep relaxation.

TAI CHI RESOURCES

- **Tai Chi Health:**
  https://www.Taichihealth.com

- **The Tree of Life Tai Chi Center:**
  https://www.treeoflifetaichi.com

- **Jake Mace Tai Chi:**
  https://www.youtube.com/watch?v=6w7IS8_UzHM&t=23s

QIGONG RESOURCES

- **Qigong Institute:**
  https://www.qigonginstitute.org
- **Spring Forest Qigong:**
  htps://www.springforestqigong.com
- **YouTube:** https://www.youtube.com/watch?v=n
  mmNWj9YtAw

SOMATIC THERAPY RESOURCES

- **Peter A. Levine, PhD:**
  https://www.somaticexperiencing.com

EXPLORATION & ENRICHMENT

"Your sense of personal well-being and enrichment lay the foundation for every other achievement in your life."

—ANTHONY ROBBINS

It is not enough to go through our days tackling our obligations and to do lists. Unfortunately, it sometimes feels like that is all we get to do before we run out of energy and time or get swept away in a wave of unwelcome distractions. There are days when it feels like we are *battling, climbing uphill,* or even *drowning*.

Is that why we are here, on this planet, at this time? I believe we are here to experience JOY, LOVE and CONNECTION. But to live fully and have a personal sense of well-being, we need to feel we are being of value, utilizing our talents, and amplifying our passions. We are here to learn and explore, to teach, to connect and to inspire. Not everyone gets it, and not everyone is born into a life where those opportunities exist. Atrocities are committed against humanity each and every day. Poverty, hatred, hunger, abuse of power, corruption and control impact many souls on this planet. It is our responsibility to be of service to those who are vulnerable. We can transform lives and inspire others by giving a little or a lot of our time and attention, by having compassion and by living an enriching life.

How can we lift someone up if we ourselves are stumbling? Forgive me for digressing again to the analogy of putting on your own oxygen mask first, but I believe it illustrates in so many ways that it is hard to give and be of service if we ourselves are depleted. We need to fill our own well before we can replenish others. In order to enhance the value or quality of something or someone, we must live enriching lives. The quality of your life depends on how well you are doing in all the essential facets of your life. These include relationships, finances, education, work, health, community, spirituality, and so on. If any of these areas are out of balance, depleted, overdrawn, or out of alignment, it is difficult to experience a sense of personal well-being. Furthermore, if one area is out of whack, it is quite possible that a domino effect will cause problems in the other areas of your life.

Creating enrichment and balance in your life means feeding all the parts of you that want to express themselves. Perhaps we can't do that all at one time, however committing to cultivating what is important to you is a first step in the right direction. This includes big bucket list things, self-development, personal goals worth attaining, and personal celebrations of accomplishments and milestones. This is the rich part of our lives that gives us joy, depth, growth, curiosity, and even courage. Enrichment is experiencing the different facets of life with passion and engagement, providing a forward momentum of self growth and full experience of life.

Enrichment is the source of our well-being and the foundation of our personal happiness. Each of us has our list of dreams and hopes. What's on that list for you personally? Is it writing, learning a language, achieving a noteworthy goal, traveling to an amazing place? Do these things get sidetracked because of your life's current circumstances? Not to worry, it happens to all of us. But remember, this is just a season of your life, and what you are enduring today will pass. Enrichment elevates our human experience and stretches us beyond the boundaries of who we are in the present moment. Each of us should be on a quest to learn more, find meaning in our experiences, and celebrate with joy and gratitude the blessings bestowed upon us.

My advice is simple and familiar. Start small. What do you want to explore or expose yourself to? What fills you up and gets you excited? What makes you extremely happy when you focus on it? Whatever it is, write it down and start doing it. There are a billion ways to live an enriching life. Your dreams propel you forward. Guard your time fiercely so that you can move towards those dreams. Set aside a day, or even an hour a week, if that's all you have. If we are constantly swept up in the drama, chaos, fear, and routine busyness, we are not running our lives, our lives are running us. Things will not change until we intentionally step away. Rise above what plays out in front of you and do not waste your time and attention on what does not serve you or your loved ones. Instead, turn your precious attention to what elevates and inspires you. Your well-being and that of others will reflect your choices.

CREATIVITY

"If you hear a voice within you say, 'You cannot paint,' then by all means paint, and that voice will be silenced."

—VINCENT VAN GOGH

Within every soul is a fountain of creativity to be explored with fervor and curiosity. Like nature, creative projects redirect our attention from the mundane and ordinary, elevating our human experience. We may not consider ourselves artists, but in fact we truly are because we are creating the story of our own lives through our dreams, actions, intentions, choices and decisions. Creativity by definition is the use of the imagination, and artistry is the way we assert that imagination in our lives, whether it be art, science, teaching, caregiving, problem solving, self-expression, devising inventions, building relationships or even parenting. Our lives are the masterpieces we work on every day.

When I was a high school student, I was very creative. I had an active imagination and a gift for story-telling. I was also very studious, good at math and visual arts, and had a keen interest in business. I had planned to go to art school and apply to Rhode Island School of Design. Instead, a series of events unfolded which led to a complete turnabout in my plans. In my junior year, I took an economic class that exposed me to Wall Street, the stock market, and how companies are run. It absolutely fascinated me and upon a visit to Wall Street, I became electrified.

At that same time, I was taking a studio art class and we were given the assignment to do a painting that evoked an emotion. I don't know why I chose the emotion *rage*, but I remember with great detail the painting I created. The painting was in vivid, intense colors. It was a closeup of an angry, scowling face with clawed hands reaching out from the canvas. In retrospect, I'll admit, it was quite disturbing. When I brought the canvas home, my parents responded by telling me to remove it from our house. I felt an overwhelming feeling of rejection as an artist. My loving and nurturing parents, and my mother in particular, were horrified by the painting. Due to this rejection, the pain of which I remember to this day, I decided to apply to business school instead of art school.

After obtaining a degree in finance and an internship with IBM, I began work in the corporate sector, learning different aspects of financial planning, accounting, budgeting, pricing and strategic planning. I was an astute learner and rose through the corporate ranks quickly. By all accounts, I had a very successful career progression, but every day I spent in this role, I questioned whether this was the right path for me, as my heart always pined for artistic work and expression.

As we all know, there is little room for creative accounting and finance. It will actually get you in trouble, and possibly thrown in jail.

In spite of my previous, painful repudiation as an artist, I continued to feed my creative soul with enrichment classes, design projects, sketching, drawing, and writing. At first, I was very guarded and created just for me. Eventually I worked up the bravery to give one of my paintings to a friend for their birthday. I slowly got over the rejection from my high school days and acknowledged that I could be an artist too.

Later in my career, I made a decision to go to night school and pursue a degree in design. This was quite daunting as I had a toddler at home and was working full time. Throughout this period there was an ongoing internal reckoning between the left and right hemispheres of my brain. I wasn't certain if it was a blessing or a curse to be so evenly balanced between the logical, reasoning side of my brain and the creative side. Typically, it felt like turmoil with each side jockeying for world domination, until one day someone said something very simple and profound:

"Why do you feel like it's a battle? Can't both sides coexist peacefully and you utilize your creativity with your logic to perform greater at every level and be more holistically attuned?"

And there you have it. It was a pivotal and life changing moment for me. It shifted the trajectory of my career, and how I approached the world. (Thank you, my dear Antoinette - xo).

Creative and enrichment experiences are engaging, challenging, and immersive, leading us to grow and expand. When we explore both the things that we are interested in as well as things we know nothing about, we grow, expand our brains, polish our skills, and ultimately become better, well rounded human beings. As long as our hearts are beating, we should be on a quest to experience as much as we can in this world.

SPARKING THE IMAGINATION

Art washes away from the soul the dust of everyday life.

—PABLO PICASSO

Just as the ordinary and mundane activities of our lives require motivation and drive, living an enriching life requires sparking the imagination. The word inspiration means *to breathe into*. Inspiration is the spark that breathes life into our imaginations so we can actualize our desires.

Nurturing the imagination is actionable and intentional. If we do not take time out to cultivate and feed our imaginations, our lives will be filled with rote to do lists, obligations, and work, leaving us feeling very unfulfilled. Sparking the imagination creates all the juiciness of our lives and gives our existence meaning and passion. This is what is referred to as the *heart of everyday living.*

Sparking the imagination comes easier to some than others. I love to brainstorm and to plan. For me, it is the most exciting part of any dream or intention because it's a blank canvas. Possibilities are limitless. If that is not your strong suit, fear not. A guide can show you the way. If you do a Google search on **ideas to spark the imagination** you will get over 17 million results. There is no shortage of inspiration for generating great visioning techniques and other ways to spark ideas to make your life more fulfilling. Here, I am introducing just a few tools that are really useful in whipping up creativity and intention to manifest a more enriching life.

VISION BOARD

A vision board is simply a pictorial representation of what you would like to manifest in your life, whether it be for a specific project or to capture your life dreams.

Using photos, words, and even materials such as fabric, wood and magazine clippings, a vision board visually represents the components of what you would like to create in the future. There are various ways to capture a vision board including poster board, a bulletin board, and even Pinterest. I use artist's sketchbooks to capture individual dreams/goals and continue to add images to them over the years. Keeping your vision board accessible and viewing it daily helps focus your mind and heart toward manifesting your dreams. Creating a vision board returns us to the creativity of our childhood, opening us to magical possibilities and wonder. It's also a fun activity to do with a group of friends. This past holiday season, my friends and I decided to make vision gingerbread houses instead of holiday cookies. What a fun and messy project! Each of us created a unique gingerbread house with all of the accoutrements of what we desired to manifest in the coming year. My gingerbread house was a barn complete with horses, and a cowgirl to represent my desire to manifest a ranch. Each person expressed so much creativity and originality in this project. By working on this project together we were able to provide support and encouragement for one another's dreams for the future. By inviting the element of play, we were accessing our childlike wonder. It certainly was a memorable experience enhanced with joy and laughter.

For more information on creating a vision board, see the field notes of this chapter.

GOALS AND DREAMS

Each of us has a treasure trove of goals and dreams for our life. Some may be simple and others outrageous. Do you spend time thinking about these goals, including why they are important to you and how they align with your values? Do you take the time to put them down on paper and set a timeframe for achieving them? Can you break these goals down into actionable steps?

GOAL SETTING EXERCISE

Take a few moments to let your goals flourish. With a single blank piece of paper, write down at least five things that you want to achieve in the coming year. These should be things that really get you excited when you think about achieving them, big or small. Think about all of the different areas of your life (relationships, work, recreation, personal development, etc.), and identify a goal for each area.

For example, *good health and well-being* always makes my annual goal list. However, I may take a different approach to achieving this goal each year. Once you have a list of goals to choose from, take the ones that resonate with you the most. On a separate piece of paper, write one of your goals. To continue with my my example of good health and well-being, I may then create a list of actionable steps to take (maybe for the next 30-60 days) and list them out:

Take impeccable care of myself

Change my habits for nourishment to include things that benefit my energy and vitality level

Develop a strength building regimen

Improve my conditions for more rest and high quality sleep

More moving, less standing still

Wear active wear more often so that I am more inclined to exercise

Drink more water daily

Do not expect to do all of these items simultaneously on Day 1, but by developing a list and having it in a visible place such as your daily or weekly planner or pinned to an inspiration board will make you more inclined to remember what your end goal is and provide a roadmap to achieve it.

Typically, we set our intentions and resolutions at the beginning of each calendar year. Some do this in ritualistic fashion on the last day of the year or New Year's Day. These intentions are consecrated by reflection on the year past and the power of the year to come. After that, what happens? Many people work diligently towards their goals as the year unfolds, but for others, good intentions fall by the wayside. Unless we are disciplined, it is easy to let the things that we did not expect overshadow or distract us from our goals. This is why it is more effective to visit our goals and dreams on a seasonal basis. With the oncoming season, such as spring, one can review the progress made over the past three months and reevaluate if your plans need any tweaking. I became familiar with this process a few years ago and for me this has produced the best outcomes for manifesting exactly what I want, despite the unexpected twists and turns that are inevitable.

Goal and dream planning interact with the neuroplasticity of our brains and wire us to think, imagine, and plan for what we want. Rather than feeling like a leaf blowing in the wind, chart out your course and the step-by-step plans to move in the direction you want to go. I have included resources and tools for goal planning in the field notes of this chapter.

KEEP AN IDEA NOTEBOOK

I envy the artists, designers, and other creative souls who carry a small notebook with them wherever they go and fill them with lovely notes, sketches, ideas, conversations, and musings. Over the years I have tried to take on this wonderful practice. Unfortunately, consistency is king and I am not disciplined enough to carry that little notebook with me everywhere I go. However, they are absolutely effective for those who commit to carrying and utilizing them. I have observed this is a more effective and frequent practice for men rather than women, perhaps because of the way we are wired. These little notebooks capture the sparks of ideas and the ruminations of the imagination that can someday lead to great companies, buildings, inventions, solutions, and brainstorms to better ourselves and our world. The fleeting thoughts and ideas we capture in these little books are there to inspire us to create or explore things in the future.

WRITING AND JOURNALING

In Chapter Five I touched on journaling as a means of self-reflection. However, it is also a great tool for sparking the imagination. Our minds and our hearts open up when we take time for reflection. Our imaginations can be stirred by brainstorming, mind mapping, and capturing ideas and free association on paper. Write down things that resonate with you and brainstorm ways to explore what tugs at your heartstrings.

DAYDREAM

In grammar school we were called out for daydreaming and staring out the window. Our teachers wanted our complete attention on what was going on in the classroom. Today, give yourself permission to daydream. Daydreaming is one of the most effective tools for sparking the imagination. When we daydream, we are shifting into a stream of consciousness state which is outside of our current conditions or life. It is a great way to escape from the stress and pressures of life and a lovely form of retreating from reality. This is an effective tool not only in sparking the imagination but in soothing ourselves during stressful times. I often daydream about living on a ranch with wide open spaces, large oak trees and lots of animals. It gives me great happiness.

Daydreams are the gateway to creativity. By detaching from our immediate situation, we are propelled to heightened problem solving as well as our potential as human beings. They allow us to rise above our current plight and seek possibility via images and forms not available to us in our routine lives. Daydreams help our minds relax and open up. I encourage you to find time to just be and daydream each and every day. Perhaps by carving out some time on a park bench or during a walk, you can kindle a dream that lights you up and makes you happy. The key is to connect with your heart, rather than with your mind so that you are projecting loving energy towards your dreams. Focus on reflecting your heart's desires rather than rumination. If you find yourself in a cerebral state, you may spiral downward and fall victim to the inner critic, the enemy of daydreaming.

EXPERIENCES – LESS STUFF, MORE JOY

Many people pursue things in life that they believe will give them lasting happiness. These include careers, money, cars, homes, jewelry, clothing, toys, and all manner of material things. It is human nature to desire and pursue what appeals to us. However exciting and fun it is to acquire and have these things, studies show that they are not directly proportional to our enduring happiness in life. At first, we are gratified by material things, but as time passes, our enthusiasm wanes and we may even find ourselves divesting ourselves of what we once coveted.

It's a fact that the more you have, the more you have to take care of. It requires energy, attention and money. When our stuff starts to fill our homes (and in particular our garages) and overflows to storage units, we are literally outgrowing our stuff. Or perhaps our stuff is outgrowing us. About a decade ago our family was making a monthly trip to the Goodwill donation center to drop off things that we no longer needed. Included in these trips were clothing, furniture, household goods, decorations, toys, sporting equipment, etc. Each time we packed up one or both of our cars, I felt a sense of guilt. We were clearly caught up in the wave of mass consumerism and instant gratification. It really got me thinking that there must be a better way.

In 2018 I decided to become a Professional Organizer after retiring from the corporate world. It became a mission for me to help educate people on how to be organized with their homes and offices, as well as the energetic implications of being weighed down by too much stuff. My area of specialty was focused on individuals going through transitions including downsizing, divorce, illness, and empty nests. The tagline of my business is Less Clutter, More Joy. By removing the clutter from people's lives, and particularly during difficult seasons of life, I was consistently observing a greater sense of liberation and freedom for my clients.

In 2019, during a life transition for my father, my husband and I decided to put my business philosophy to work in our own lives and promptly made the decision to downsize from our four bedroom home to a 1,600 square foot condominium with relatively little storage. In the process, we curated the few sentimental and important things we wanted to keep, selling 85% of our belongings in an estate sale. We had collected stuff over our twenty-five years together and just like that, it was all gone. As a result, we have been able to focus on living a very full and enriching life unencumbered by belongings that get dusty, worn, require maintenance or are forgotten on some hidden shelf or storage area. Today, everything we have is functional and well loved.

The richness of our lives should be measured by our biggest assets, that is, our health and well-being. Without both of these, it really does not matter how much money or possessions you have. Reflected to us all through 2020 and the Coronavirus pandemic is the fact that it doesn't matter who you are or what you have, we are all equally exposed and at risk from a non-discriminatory virus. Taking care of ourselves and our loved ones become our priority. Suddenly, it doesn't really matter what you are wearing, driving, and buying because the focus has shifted to care and concern for our worldwide population. Our spending patterns have also shifted from trivial things to essentials and items of comfort in the midst of the unknown.

Experiences, rather than things, provide key elements for our well-being. The people we share unique adventures and journeys with are indelibly etched in our minds, connecting us to each other. Our experiences become our memories, our stories, and possibly our incentive for inspiring others. Our stuff just cannot do that. Our stuff bogs us down and keeps us tethered to caring for it rather than ourselves. It's great to have stuff and enjoy our stuff while we have it, but experiences offer us joy, enrichment, and fun for the long haul.

EXPLORATION AND ENRICHMENT – LA DOLCE VITA

There is nothing more depleting creatively than when we are stuck in routine habits and predictable chaos. How can we be creative when we are overwhelmed, dealing with stress, crisis and trauma? When we are on autopilot or consumed with stress, we take the path of least resistance and fall back on familiar comfort zones. Surprisingly, this is the optimal time to liberate ourselves and gain a new perspective. When we are depleted of our life force, connecting with an activity that inspires, excites, or even scares us, catapults us out of our conditions and makes us feel alive.

The year my mother passed away, I planned a retreat in Italy with my girlfriend Melinda. After all I had been through, I was a mere shadow of myself. My vitality was depleted, the tank was empty, and I had not yet even begun the grieving part of her death. I knew that our trip to Italy would primarily be centered on the organic cooking school in Tuscany we had enrolled in. That vision alone pulled me forward. What was unexpected and perhaps the delight of the trip were the enrichment experiences I didn't anticipate that were interwoven with our main plan. These experiences actually began well before we left when we decided to take Italian lessons at a church in San Diego's Little Italy. Each week we sat in a classroom enunciating Italian phrases. I had taken Italian in college, but over the years the language merged with the Spanish I had studied in high school. Learning the language all over again created an energy of excitement within me that spoke of *possibilta'* and made me enthusiastic about what was to come.

When we arrived in Italy, we behaved like typical tourists and visited the duomos and museos. They were just as I imagined while studying architecture and art history in design school. However, the experiences that truly resonated with me were these delightfully unexpected things:

- Savoring a different flavor of gelato twice a day
- Visiting the cellar of a restaurant in Sienna with cheeses bountifully spread out before us and dancing to pop music at our table
- Stopping at gas stations for espresso
- Visiting an organic farm to learn about beekeeping and everything there is to know about honey
- Smelling the intoxicatingly sweet scent of the acacia blooms in the courtyard of our inn
- Doing an olive oil tasting and picking olives (which is not an easy task)
- Running up and down the hills of Tuscany through grapevines and olive groves, the fields vibrantly alive with red poppies
- Attending the Opera La Traviata in Florence and dinner afterwards at midnight
- Riding bicycles on the walled city of Luca on a cool spring afternoon, feeling alive and free with the wind on my face
- Taking the *Tour of Hell* in Florence (yes, this really is a thing)
- Enjoying smiley face cappuccinos and croissants in Umbria
- A nine-course luncheon with wine pairings at a winery in Spello

These are all examples of la dolce vita, the sweet life. Each brought me back to myself through connection with sensory experiences that immersed me in something so out of the ordinary from my normal life. In some ways they seemed transcendental. My spirits were elevated by the exposure to new things in a time when I so desperately needed to be lifted.

During these experiences I also learned that you do not need to have a passport and travel halfway around the world to be enriched and renewed. I have developed a relentless curiosity that pushes me to seek out these experiences wherever I go. In most instances, I don't even need to leave home. These enrichment experiences are everywhere to be found, even in our own backyards. I intentionally cultivated a plan to seek them out each and every week, and more so when the global pandemic limited our travel to other places.

What experiences await you in your backyard? Perhaps there is a potter that will teach you how to throw pots? Have you visited a community garden? What about the botanical gardens? Recently my husband and I took a bike ride to Balboa Park in San Diego, home of the World Famous San Diego Zoo. We spent the day visiting all the nooks and crannies of the park that we had never known existed. We have been there a thousand times and yet had a brand new experience that day. Is there an animal refuge near you where you can learn about endangered or rescued animals? What about a local brewer or cidery? A lesson on how Kombucha is made? A glassblower? How about a planetarium? If you haven't taken a cooking class, it's a great way to spend an afternoon or evening with friends. You also make new connections which are so essential in these days of isolation, working from home, and an overwhelming nonstop news cycle.

As I close out this chapter, the seventh and final foundational element to the Art of Retreating, I am reflecting on the fact that our lives are really a woven tapestry of all of the enriching experiences we have from childhood until we take our last breath. Our experiences would not be as meaningful without the connection of others with whom we share them. We are bonded to each other through our fun, adventurous experiences as well as life's most difficult chapters.

A final personal story regarding shared experiences. My mother loved Christmas more than any other holiday. She decorated every square inch of her house inside and out. She shopped for presents for family and friends throughout the year and these wrapped gifts extended so far from beneath the tree, that there was typically nowhere to walk.

During the final few months of her life, she sensed that she would not live to see Christmas that year. While in the hospital, she wrote out an extensive Christmas gift list and sent my sister out into New York City on a massive gift buying excursion. Each name on the list had a specific gift penned next to it. Her list included her sisters, her children, her grandchildren, my father, her sons- and daughters-in-law and all of her friends. My sister dutifully shopped for all of these gifts between visits to see my mom at Sloan Kettering Cancer Center. She painstakingly wrapped all of the gifts and shipped them as instructed back to my parents' home in Tennessee. It was a massive undertaking.

My mom was escorted home on an Angel flight provided by my father's company so that she could be in her own home for hospice. When my mom's journey brought her home, the gifts began arriving. My parents had been in New York City since Thanksgiving when my mom had to be hospitalized. There were no Christmas decorations up at the house. To honor my mother, my siblings and I knew that we had to decorate the house with lights and a Christmas tree, despite how we felt regarding the holiday festivities.

In her final days, neighbors and friends learned of her return home and brought over food and holiday decorations. One special friend put a large angel on my parents' front lawn which became a symbol of love and hope during a dark time. During hospice, the week before Christmas, many of my mom's friends and neighbors gathered on the lawn and began singing Christmas carols outside of her bedroom window. With the window wide open, my mom sat up in bed, probably for the last time, and delighted at the songs being sung to her. Both children and adults were singing through their tears. Each person had the opportunity to step up to the window to say a few words. She directed her sisters and my father to hand out the gifts that she selected for those dear friends as they said their goodbyes. Everyone was dumbfounded that through all of her suffering and pain over these past few months she had her attention focused on the people she loved.

In the spirit of love and connection, my mom's generosity and giving heart poured forth to her loved ones right up until the moment she took her last breath. The enriching experience of selflessness, connection and joy filled the hearts of those who knew and loved her and left an indelible mark. It was a powerful and profound experience and reminds me of the preciousness of each moment of our lives. My mom only lived seventy-one years but oh how rich and colorful the tapestry of her life was.

How intricate and vibrant your tapestry becomes is up to you.

FIELD NOTES FOR EXPLORATION AND ENRICHMENT:

HOW TO MAKE A VISION BOARD:

- **Christine Kane Blog**: https://christinekane.com/how-to-make-a-vision-board/#sthash.iNO5AzHG.uiuotyNc.dpbs

GOAL AND DREAM PLANNING:

- **Cultivate What Matters Powersheets** and planning with Lara Casey: https://cultivatewhatmatters.com
- *Everything is Figureoutable* by Marie Forleo: https://www.marieforleo.com/2016/05/everything-is-figureoutable/

IDEA NOTEBOOKS:

- **Moleskine** — The classic iconic notebook used by many professionals: https://us.moleskine.com/notebooks/classic/0201-2
- Search the internet for: small slim paper notebook to get a wide variety of notebooks in size, color and weight.

12

OUR ROOTS AND CONNECTION

"Individually we are one drop, together we are the ocean."

—UNKNOWN

The Art of Retreating is a guide to caring deeply for ourselves throughout our lives so that we can live from the wellspring of our truest and fullest selves. When we are in retreat, we are intentionally stepping away, in solitude, in most cases. From that place of self-compassion, self love and time alone, we return as enriched and energetic beings.

Equally essential to stepping away is stepping back into your life, reconnecting with loved ones and your community. When you have taken the intentional time and space to refill your own well, you bring energy and vitality to share with others. In doing so, you can inspire, uplift and be the example of love and hope for those around you.

There is an invisible network of connection that exists between all the souls that express themselves on this planet. It may not be visible to the naked eye, but it is there. Empaths know this very well because we sense the feelings of others around us, and even of total strangers. The actions, thoughts, words, and deeds spoken by one of us ripple out and affect all others. The way we express ourselves in the world either raises all boats or sinks them.

Essential to all life is this hidden network of energy. There are beautiful examples of this at work in nature. The mycelium network of mushrooms and fungi that exist beneath the ground we walk upon is one of them. Mycelium means *"more than one."* Illustrations show just how widespread and vast these networks can be. Dense superhighways of incredibly complex structures release enzymes (energy) simultaneously decomposing materials and providing nutrition for the ecosystems of the planet. This marvelous collective is essential to plant life by transforming nutrients into usable materials for the benefit of other life forms.

Another example of this invisible network in nature is the relationship between trees. I have been fascinated with trees all my life, a passion cultivated in childhood on long walks in the woods with my father. In addition to reading about trees as a girl, I have always been particularly curious about the Tree of Life as a symbol in religion and spirituality. In a bestselling book entitled, The Hidden Life of Trees: What They Feel, How They Communicate, author Peter Wolhlleben writes about forests being superorganisms of unique individuals. His observation is that trees are far more alert, social, sophisticated, and even intelligent, than we thought.[15] It is through their root systems that they are deeply connected and communicate with each other. When one tree dies, the others around it usually die as well. I have seen this phenomena firsthand at the Torrey Pines Reserve in California. I have walked the trails of the reserve for more than twenty years. Over time I've witnessed a beautiful grove of the endangered trees shrivel up and die simultaneously. Of course there were environmental factors at play, but the beautiful vibrant spirit of that grove evacuated all at once and left behind a skeletal collection of trunks devoid of life.

Yet another example of the connections found in nature is the diversity of the plants and trees that can coexist with one another in a full display of abundance and bounty. The wildflowers and ferns grow at the foot of the redwoods each in their individual and collective

15 *The Hidden Life of Trees: What They Feel, How They Communicate* by Peter Wohlleben, 2015: https://www.goodreads.com/book/show/28256439-the-hidden-life-of-trees

glory. They do not compete with one another, however they simply express themselves and benefit from their relationship to one another. These examples of symbiotic life can teach us a lot about our own invisible connections with one another. The year 2020 was a global lesson in coexistence and diversity. Either we find a way, as nature teaches us, to be symbiotic and supportive of one another or we shall all perish.

I'd like to think of the invisible network of energy between all souls as the *rooted heart*. Like mycelium, our hearts are not visible to the outside world, but they are certainly there below the surface guiding and connecting us in ways we do not even understand. Our hearts either connect with one another or they do not. When we close or cut off our hearts due to pain and suffering, we choke the very lifeforce and vitality that sustains us and our relationships. When we withhold our love from one another because we disapprove, are displeased or disagree, we isolate ourselves and endanger our own vitality and wellbeing. The individual on the receiving end feels this experience as well.

During the pandemic, humanity has undergone a giant experiment. We have been asked by our nation's leaders to *separate* for the survival of our population because of a virus. We all feel the effects of the challenges this has presented. We are social and loving creatures by nature and we want nothing more than to be together. Each of us wants to see family and friends;

to hug our loved ones; to shake the hand or pat the back of a colleague or neighbor. We desperately miss our elderly family members, and they desperately miss us. We are longing for the collective experiences of sports events, concerts, theater, movies, museums and community events because our experiences are amplified when we are together. These are the experiences that bond us together and elevate us. We are wired to be together and rooted in the heart.

The experiences of 2020 have brought us together in some respects, and vastly polarized us in other ways. We are bumping up against our edges as we learn from both the isolation as well as too much time spent together. Our tolerance levels are deteriorating. The separation and divorce rate is significantly on the rise, as are the rates of suicide and depression.

Being rooted in connection is essential for the survival of humanity as we move into a very different world post pandemic. It is up to each of us to understand how essential our connectivity is to the future of our relationships, our nations, and our planet. The lessons have unfolded before our eyes, the dramas have played out, and the repercussions are rippling out around the globe. Our responsibility is to learn, to grow, and to rise above our current circumstances. In the process of elevating yourself, your example raises others up as well. It must be enacted in the spirit of love, compassion, empathy, and forgiveness.

FORGIVENESS

*"The practice of forgiveness is our most important
contribution to the healing of the world."*
—MARIANNE WILLIAMSON

In our collective experience, each of us have faced
hurts, heartbreak, and have been victimized in one form
or another by people we love and trust. Whether we
consciously are aware or not, we too have been the
reason for other people's pain and suffering. At the root
of our suffering can be misaligned expectations, jealousy,
competition, power, abuse, and meanspiritedness. When
we pour our hearts and generosity out into the world
and don't receive back what we expect, we are let down
and experience pain. When someone we love breaks our
trust, our heart breaks on some level.

Whether it is our pain, or the pain of another, holding onto this burden is like carrying a bag of rocks on our
backs. It weighs us down, causing discomfort and blocking us from moving forward. We are very much aware
that the bag of rocks is there but something prevents
us from letting it go and liberating ourselves from the
hold it has on us. The only way to move forward unencumbered is to acknowledge the emotion and practice
forgiveness. We forgive first for ourselves and then for
each other. We forgive ourselves *"for-giving"* and not

getting what we expected in return. We forgive others so that we can let go of the emotions that are toxic to our own well-being and for the blessing of another. This does not mean those who have done wrong by us are not accountable for their actions, but that their actions no longer have a hold on our lives.

Because we are connected, the act of forgiveness is a very integral part of self love and compassion. Without the perception to see toxic experience for what it was, acknowledge our own role in the pain and suffering, and liberate ourselves on the other side, we are stuck in the drama of what we endured, frequently living it over and over again. Forgiveness requires a high level of grace and is not an easy thing to do. Sometimes, it takes a long time to forgive. When people that we love and hold in high esteem disappoint us or break our trust, the wounds run deep. The longer these wounds fester, the more suffering we endure. Forgiveness offers us a guiding hand out of the experience.

I have seen and experienced the power of forgiveness both firsthand and for my loved ones. I have supported seven family members through heartbreak and healing on their individual journeys. Each of these people, who I adore, are now living with joy, peace, resilience and optimism for their future. They also are using their own experiences to better the lives of others through service.

It is not only personal and family relationships that create opportunities for forgiveness. I have endured great pain and suffering because of the actions of others in a toxic work environment. I invested my time, my heart, and money into a business. I came to understand that the motives of the individuals in charge were drastically different than my own. We were completely out of alignment even though I believed we were interested in the same end goals. In addition, the work environment was a toxic, emotional muck of egos, power, and narcissism. I eventually quit and walked away from four years of my hard work as well as a large chunk of money my husband and I invested in the company. It took a while to reorient myself after that extremely stressful time and to forgive both myself and the actions of the executive team. I acknowledged my role in all of the drama that unfolded. I realized I had turned my own power and agency over to others that I trusted. In retrospect, I see that I was there to also be an example to the others who were victimized and deceived and to assist them in moving onto something better. While I did not recover all of our investment, nor am I thrilled that I gave up four years of my precious life to go through that experience, I do know that it has made me a more compassionate leader. I no longer feel anger and hostility towards the people that took advantage of me and others. In fact, through my forgiveness process, I am now able to bless each of them.

Forgiveness is a tough assignment. When you allow yourself to feel the pain and other emotions brought about by another person's actions, you can free yourself from the weighty bag of rocks, restoring yourself with the release and wisdom that you gain. Let it go. In the world we live in today, tolerance is a rare and much needed attribute in our interactions with one another. Rather than getting all riled up by what other people think and say, allow for the freedom of expression of differing viewpoints. We broaden our perspective and insights, and compassionately understand that the experiences that each individual has endured, have colored their view of the world. Their formative core beliefs stem from how they were raised and what they have chosen to believe in the span of their lifetime. Why should we make our lives more difficult by reacting to what other people say or do? Practice forgiveness and tolerance throughout your life and you will be the better for it, both for yourself and for those around you.

ISOLATION AND SIX FEET APART

Statistics are available on the effects of social isolation related to the pandemic and the rise in mental health issues, domestic violence, and substance abuse and addiction.[16] The population of people experiencing homelessness has increased significantly in San Diego

16 National Institute of Health: https://www.ncbi.nim.nih.gov

and other urban centers due to mental illness, job loss, and expanding poverty. There is also a rise in depression for everyone, especially seniors, due to social isolation and loneliness. These trends are of great concern for the well-being of our society today and beyond.

Prevention is the key to reducing the harm and very serious side effects of the pandemic. We are in this for the long haul, or at least for the foreseeable future. Despite quarantines, social distancing, and isolation, there are things that we can employ to reduce anxiety and build resilience. Mostly, it is about maintaining our connections, and we do need to be creative to do that. Here is a list of the basics, with more detail provided in the field notes of this chapter.

- Make it a point to spend quality time with family doing fun or creative things
- Maintain social connections through technology
- Create a structure to your day (make a plan)
- Get outdoors in nature
- Exercise
- Volunteer
- Plan a social activity with friends and keep your distance
- Engage in mindful and intellectual activities

- Visit elderly family members in person yet from afar
- Check in on friends through phone calls and video chat rather than through texts and emails
- Know the signs of depression and other psychiatric symptoms; seek help immediately through your doctor, mental health experts, and support organizations

October 10th is World Mental Health Awareness Day which was established to increase awareness and advocacy for the importance of mental health, and to minimize the stigma of mental health issues. I believe that if you have not personally been rocked in some way during 2020, you are superhuman. My personal mental stress revolved around the well-being of my children, the care and security of my father who is living with dementia, and the lack of clarity for consistent, reliable information regarding the pandemic and what steps we should be taking. No longer having a job also weighed heavily on me. It has been my faith and resilience that has sustained me, along with the support of my husband. The writing of this book has been extremely cathartic, providing an outlet for my voice and the means of caring for myself.

I cannot emphasize enough that if you are suffering in ANY way from mental health concerns as a direct result of the pandemic, isolation, or ongoing issues in your life, PLEASE reach out for help right now. There are many people experiencing exactly what you are. You are not alone. Remember, we are all connected and I feel that strong connection with you. There are amazing resources to support and uplift you.

If you are in desperate need and in deep despair, contact the universal suicide prevention hotline immediately: 800-273-8255

There are other general resources of support in the field notes, and I encourage you to research resources in your geographic area. Among us are amazing, skilled and loving experts to walk with you on this journey and light the way back from darkness.

WHEN ENOUGH IS ENOUGH

Equally trying as isolation is the stress and anxiety of spending too much time with a loved one because of quarantine orders. Being with one or more people twenty-four hours a day, seven days a week is an extremely challenging situation even when you get along well. It's important to get some separation time in one form or another so that you don't drive each other crazy. My mom's last words to me were, "Know when enough is enough." At the time, I wasn't really sure what she meant. Over and over, this phrase keeps showing up in my life. When you feel like it's too much, know when enough is enough and step away. It may be your spouse, your children or your roommate that you need to retreat from. Our tolerance levels vary and so do our levels of independence. Each of us needs alone time. My husband and I are best friends and enjoy doing most everything together, but even we were challenged by the lack of solitude and freedom to do something just for ourselves.

The combination of stress, financial strain, uncertainty, unemployment, death of loved ones, homeschooling children, working from home, and mental health issues have put significant strain on relationships.

According to statistics provided by the Substance Abuse and Mental Health Services Administration, the lockdowns and quarantine have increased the rate of child abuse and neglect by five times.[17] Intimate partner violence is expected to dramatically rise as stay-at-home orders force victims to stay in dangerous situations. Children staying home from school who are food insecure are not getting essential nutrition usually provided through school lunch programs. Counselors

17 Substance Abuse and Mental Health Services: https://www.SAMHSA.gov

and teachers are unable to observe signs of abuse and report them to authorities. Many at-risk families are unable to access technology to keep up with remote learning. These beautiful souls are falling through the cracks without a safety net. They are isolated from their support systems, safety nets, and communities. The issues they experience today will ripple through society and all of us in the future. If you or family members are suffering from any of these issues, know that it is possible to get the support you need.

You do not need to stay in a dangerous or abusive situation. Recently my daughter told me a story about a young woman who was the victim of domestic violence in her home. She finally worked up the nerve to reach out for help, even under the watchful eye of her abuser. She called the local domestic violence hotline and asked to order a pepperoni pizza. The astute operator who answered the call asked her some basic questions while going along with the charade and also asked the woman for her address to deliver the pizza. Rather than a pizza delivery, the police showed up. That brave young woman knew when enough was enough and courageously took the steps to remove herself from the horror of her situation with ingenuity and calm.

Our community networks need to be aware of the impact that the confluence of these circumstances can have on vulnerable individuals and unstable households. Together we must provide alternative solutions to address the social services drastically needed. Enough is enough. If you find yourself in the position of domestic violence and abuse or know someone that is, please contact one of the SAMHSA resources provided in the field notes of this chapter.

OUR ROOTED HEART COMMUNITY

"All shallow roots must be uprooted because they are not deep enough to sustain you."
—A COURSE IN MIRACLES

I would like to end this chapter on a high note, amidst all of the turmoil and trouble that constantly swirls around us. We see a great deal of drama playing out in politics, the media, and on social media. While it's important to be informed, I challenge you to disengage from the drama, the bandwagon, and polarity that is unfolding. There is a leading cast of characters playing their roles. There are *movement* leaders. There are those with the voices who wish to be heard.

When you really think about it, unless you know a person intimately well, you do not know what motivates them. You may not understand their agenda. You also do not know what their value system is. All you really know and have agency over is your own authentic self, including your own values.

My role is certainly not to polarize nor is it to engage on the world stage of this drama. I have strong positions and viewpoints on all matters that are aligned with my morals, values, and my heart. For me, it is about listening and observing what is going on without getting swept up in it. My role is to see, learn, understand, and grow. Hopefully I will expand my viewpoint and perspective in the process.

It was helpful for me to have a mindfulness meditation counselor reframe this experience for me that we so often experience. I'd like to share it with you here.

- Envision yourself as an observer, with a physical countenance similar to that of quartz, in which light can still penetrate but with a definitive boundary that nothing else can enter.
- View everything in your daily life, the drama, challenges, experiences, things happening on the world stage, as a storm that is blowing by.
- Be the observer, but not part of the storm.
- Be the calm eye of the storm. In this way, we are mindful that we can observe what plays out before us without becoming part of it, or possibly even collaterally damaged.

I often invoke this simple mindful meditation when something disrupts my peace of mind. It is helpful to know that whatever I am observing shall pass like the storm and I can mindfully remain unscathed.

My daily mission is to love and uplift, inspire, and encourage. My motive is to see the light when others see only darkness. My actions include praying for humanity, for possibility, for connected spirit, and for symbiosis for our communities. I am an optimist and I believe from the ashes we will rise.

- How do you see yourself and your role in the dynamic story of the evolution of society?
- What can you do to enhance the lives of others and be of service?
- Can your time and attention be focused on your rooted heart community so that you can lift up just one other person?
- Are there places and spaces to include altruism in your daily activities?
- Can you volunteer to pack food, or give desperately needed blood?
- Can you take to the streets and hand out provisions to the homeless?
- Can you just smile broadly at a stranger?

Learn about special needs and then go do something to elevate your community.

In nature, the act and experience of "helping" is reciprocal and you will receive as much as you give. *The power of compassion is alchemic and research shows compassion and altruism provide more sustained happiness for the giver than any material things.*[18]

In serving others, we often find our community. This sense of belonging and communion encourages us to show up as the very best of our authentic selves. When we can no longer carry our burdens, our community carries them for us. Our community makes us laugh out loud and provides a shoulder or two to cry on. Our connections teach us to be living love. We need each other not only to get through the difficult stuff, but to live full enriching lives. Our rooted heart connections are transformational and allow us to achieve our highest potential in the spirit of joy.

18 The Center for Compassion and Altruism Research and Education, Stanford University: http://ccare.stanford.edu/video/campus-conversations-on-compassion/

FIELD NOTES ON CONNECTION AND RESOURCES FOR COMMUNITY SUPPORT

TIPS FOR PREVENTING LONELINESS AND ISOLATION

Maintain your connections — Even if you have to modify the way in which you visit with loved ones, continue to reach out and connect with them as often as possible. Spend time outside with family, call your friends for real conversation, go for a walk or hike with a friend, go visit the elderly (even if it's from outside a window).

Social Media platforms — For those who are tech savvy, utilize Facetime, Skype, Zoom, Uberconference, or any other platform which allow you to be face-to-face with your community. Check in often with loved ones.

Help others — If you are healthy, volunteer to deliver food to those who are homebound or distribute food at the local food bank or Salvation Army. Give blood. There is a shortage of blood due to fewer blood donors during the pandemic. Volunteer to watch your friends' children so that they can have a break. Deliver food and medication to the elderly.

Structure each and every day — Structure your entire day so that you have a purpose. Maintain a daily schedule with activities that are physically, mentally and spiritually challenging. If you work from home, get up and take breaks. Get outside for exercise or a walk. Limit television and excessive social media surfing. Instead declutter and organize your home, teach yourself new hobbies, learn an instrument or a new language.

Incorporate challenging physical and mental activities — Equally as beneficial for mood and cognition, engage in challenging activities, take an online exercise class, read something different than you typically read, take up cooking. Meditate, practice Tai Chi or Qigong.

Go out in nature — Expose yourself to natural sunlight which benefits mood, provides essential Vitamin D and lifts your spirit. Take a brisk walk and benefit from seeing other people even if they are strangers. You will feel less isolated.

Pay attention to your emotions — As discussed, emotions come and go. Check in with yourself to honestly acknowledge what you are feeling. Practice breathing techniques, meditation, journaling, emoting, dancing and other forms of dynamic movement to circulate the energy through you. Take a time out if you feel yourself escalating in a heated conversation. Take a nap. Reach out for support if you feel yourself dealing with ongoing anxiety, depression or other negative emotions such as anger.

FIND YOUR ROOTED HEART COMMUNITY

- Seek out a church or faith-based group that resonates with your spiritual beliefs
- Find a hiking group through your local sporting good store bulletin board or city or county websites.
- Join a yoga group; a meditation community; a Tai Chi or Qigong group - each of these benefit the body, mind and spirit and can be found online worldwide.
- Join a networking group in an area of interest, whether social or professional.
- Join a travel group
- Research clubs and activities in your community. Check the back of local community newsletters and bulletin boards in your favorite coffee shop
- Join a band or choir
- Connect with a group of runners, cyclists, or walkers and get moving
- Join a young singles or professionals club
- Volunteer for every amazing organization that you can so that you be of service to people who desperately need your support and attention.
- Become a youth mentor
- Start a neighborhood watch group

- Mix up your collection of friends so that you are graced with the wisdom and experience of those older than you, as well as the energy and enthusiasm of those who are younger.
- Play with children

MENTAL HEALTH RESOURCES

SAMHSA Resources:

- **SAMHSA's National Helpline — 1-800-662-HELP (4357)**
  SAMHSA's National Helpline is a free, confidential, 24/7, 365-day-a-year treatment referral and information service (in English and Spanish) for individuals and families facing mental and/or substance use disorders.

- **Addiction Technology Transfer Center (ATTC)** offers a session on Addiction Recovery and Intimate Violence https://healtheknowledge.org/course/view.php?id=18

- **The National Hispanic and Latino ATTC** recorded a webinar this February on the "Intersection of Domestic Violence or Intimate Partner Violence and Addiction" https://attcnetwork.org/centers/national-hispanic-and-latino-attc/product/intersection-domestic-violence-or-intimate

- **Substance Abuse Treatment and Domestic Violence** — Quick Guide for Clinicians Based on TIP 25 https://store.samhsa.gov/product/Substance-Abuse-Treatment-and- Domestic-Violence/sma15-3583

- **The National Center on Domestic Violence, Trauma & Mental Health**, a SAMHSA partner, recently released: Supporting Survivors' Access to Substance Use Disorder and Mental Health Services During the COVID-19 Emergency http://www.nationalcenterdvtraumamh.org/2020/03/covid-19-resources-for-advocates/

Other non-SAMHSA Resources:

- **Crisis Response Network** - Grief and Loss https://www.crisisnetwork.org/find-help/behavioral-health-conditions/grief-and-loss/

- **Grief Resource Network** https://www.griefresourcenetwork.com/crisis-center/hotlines/

- **National Center for State Courts:** https://www.ncsc.org/topics/children-families-and-elders/marriage-divorce-and-custody/resource-guide

- **National Domestic Violence Hotline** Phone number: 1-800-799-SAFE (7233)

- **National Family Solutions** - Divorce Help and Resources
  https://www.nationalfamilysolutions.com/divorce-help/

- **The National Institute on Drug Abuse**
  https://www.drugabuse.gov/publications/principles-drug-addiction-treatment-research-based-guide-third-edition/resources

- **The National Network to Eliminate Domestic Violence**
  https://nnedv.org

- **National Prevention Resources**
  https://nasadad.org/prevention-resources/

- **Department of Justice, Office of Women's Health**
  Resources on Domestic Violence

- **Prevent Child Abuse America**

- Coronavirus Resources & Tips for Parents, Children & Others

- **Stronghearts Native Helpline**
  1-844-762-8483

- **Suicide Prevention Hotllne**
  1-800-273-8255

13

INTENTIONS AND LASTING CHANGE

"May we grow back not to what was, but instead towards what we can become."
—FROM RADICI STUDIOS

Our minds and bodies possess magnificent intelligence to heal themselves. In order to successfully create a healing state that will endure, we need to affirm our commitment to ourselves by accessing relaxation and self compassion. Restoration and renewal require ongoing diligence and awareness which I refer to as *inspired momentum.* Inspired momentum is the energy behind the motivation to cultivate and remain in a place of peacefulness and calmness no matter what is going on around you. This is a disciplined practice of love for yourself cultivated like any habit through repetition.

When we go on a vacation or a retreat, we typically feel so wonderful and renewed by the time we are returning home. Why do we feel so good and how do we maintain that elevated level of joy, relaxation, peace and inspiration when we return to our daily life? I believe the reason we feel so good is that we have stepped out of our daily routine and opened ourselves to something unfamiliar which broadens our perspective of the world. We try new things, meet new people, and expose ourselves to new possibilities. In addition, we give ourselves *permission* to relax and unwind during this time; something we may not always create space for in the nonstop treadmill of our lives.

In the United States, the average amount of vacation offered to employees is two weeks a year. How distressing that we are wired for only two weeks of downtime during an entire year of personal and work demands. It's up to us to cultivate micro vacations or retreats throughout the year to elevate our well-being. By implementing the practices I've outlined in this book, we create inspired momentum and motivation to live at this elevated level of joy, even when it is through the difficult seasons of life.

When we return home from a vacation or escape, we are full of energy, enthusiasm, and determination to make lasting changes in our lives but the light of enthusiasm frequently wanes as we find ourselves dealing with the same or even new challenges that require our time and attention. Frequently, the emotional toll sets in and we find ourselves on the rollercoaster again. There are powerful ways to keep our intentions alive and rise above the habits of the past. We all have the power to decide.

SET INTENTIONS

You can't stick with an intention if you have not set one. In Chapters Five and Nine I talk a lot about self reflection and capturing your goals. Setting intentions is the practice of listening to what your mind, body, and spirit need to nourish, sustain, and inspire you. No one can do this for you as it emanates from your heart and authentic self. Write your intentions down and keep them in a place where you will see them daily. I capture my intentions in my goal planner and glance at them every morning. They are a reminder to me of what is important in my life and keep me from getting distracted by trivial things.

It's really important to prioritize your intentions so that you have clarity and a plan. When we take on too much or find ourselves overloaded with commitments, knowing what is most important to us provides a road-map to action. When we prioritize our guiding goals, we are less inclined to feel unmoored. If things are very intense, it's helpful to just know what your next steps are. If you don't know what they are, they will present themselves. A bit of the anxiety and stress are alleviated when you break things down into bitesize actionable steps. I have marched through some pretty daunting circumstances by assuring myself that today I just have to get through this one thing, and tomorrow I will focus on another thing, and so on. Even when we can't see what the final outcome will be, if we deal with what is squarely in front of us today, we are a step closer to getting through the storm.

Our priorities will also change with time. Just like a navigation app, we are frequently required to recalculate our route. Know in your heart that this is okay. There are many ways to move roadblocks or navigate through obstacles. The reprioritization may hold valuable lessons and show us what we would not have otherwise seen. We are never really lost.

It is natural for our intentions to change and develop over time. Find the right intentions for the season you are in. Are you trying to achieve goals for yourself that are nearly impossible for your current circumstances? While it is great to have big goals and a bucket list, if the things you are pursuing are not optimized to align with your current conditions, you may be spending a great deal of energy with no progress which can lead to frustration and possibly giving up. I will give you an example from my own life.

I have always wanted a ranch since I can remember. One day, I happened to find the property of my dreams. I spent a great deal of time obsessing over it and chasing this dream. During this season of my life, my father was diagnosed with soft tissue cancer and had to go to New York for treatment and surgery. His diagnosis and treatment came on the heels of my mother's journey with cancer, culminating in her death. In addition, my husband and I were both working full time in the corporate world and our children were in colleges in other parts of the country. My husband was not in any position to retire from his job since he was the main breadwinner of our family. The circumstances for buying and running a ranch were not ideal.

Because I wanted this dream so much, I ignored all the basic conditions of my life at the time which were not optimized to buy or run a ranch. I had a lot on my plate. Still, I put six months of my time and detailed attention into acquiring this property, including due diligence, business plan, vision board, business partner and financing arrangements. I flew off to New York on a cold February day to be by my father's side for his seven hour surgery and stayed for two weeks with my sister during his very difficult recovery. While I was there, I learned that another buyer had made an offer on the ranch. I was completely devastated because I had invested so much time, effort and heart into this project. My heart felt broken and it took me a long time to recover. In retrospect, it was really all about timing.

Knowing what intentions to set for yourself in the season that you are currently in takes practice and discernment. Sometimes it requires letting go or tabling our desires for the future. There is an art to this as we balance our endeavors between what we believe is good for us and what truly is good for us *now*. Keep all of your intentions alive in your heart because they are the dreams that enrich our lives. Ask yourself what intentions make sense and support you the most in the season you are in.

EXPERIMENT WITH THE SEVEN PRACTICES

Creating lasting change is a messy business. It is not a straightforward path, but straightforward paths are overrated. They are predictable, boring and uninspiring. The art of retreating requires us to grow and challenge ourselves as we meet head on with the unexpected. This is a hero's journey. There are going to be surprises along the way. Trust me, this year alone, I've personally had a LOT of surprises. When I do encounter something I was not expecting, I challenge myself to deal with the circumstances with grace and from a place of centeredness, which is not always easy. The beauty of encountering difficult things in your life is that the more times you do, the more proficient you become. Practice breeds mastery.

Try a variety of ways to find your oasis and build resilience and calm in the wake of your experiences. Experiment with some of the different methods I've shared. You'll find that some are good for triage and others are good for ongoing support and sustenance. Develop your own techniques from the foundation I've outlined and use the tools that work for you. Being present and mindful creates a good environment for assessment and discernment. Create the arsenal of tools that will support your personal journey.

BE KIND AND LOVING WITH YOURSELF

Our human nature is compassion, yet many of us are the least compassionate with ourselves. We are everlasting souls in a limited physical body, experiencing a limited human life. Each of us is doing the best that we can. Self love and self compassion are the most important components for success in the long haul. When we make a mistake, or when we fall back into old patterns that don't support us, the most important thing we can do is forgive ourselves and let go. When we do this, we can move forward again, even if it means starting over. While we are resistant to change, we really are changing in every moment. Don't give up on yourself and your amazing magnificence. You can heal yourself and rise to help lift others.

SEEK COMMUNITY

Being accountable to ourselves is one thing, however being accountable to others is a whole different ball game. In Chapter Twelve I discussed the importance of connection and being rooted to others in our hearts. We are all connected and each of our actions affect all others on this planet, whether we are consciously aware of this or not. Having a community can establish the best conditions for lasting change and success. We also share in each other's successes. Rooted heart community is inspiring and uplifting and always there to support us when we fall. When like-minded people understand where you are coming from and what your aspirations are, they will bond together to ensure you don't stray too far from your path and arrive at your destination.

Have an accountability partner (a friend or a family member) or even a group to keep you aligned with your intentions. There is power in numbers and together we can support each other and keep each other on track. Small networking groups are great for this, and you can check in weekly with one another in a thirty to forty minute roundtable call.

REFLECT PERIODICALLY ON YOUR LIFE

Periodically reexamining where you are, where you've been, and where you are going, are powerful navigation tools. Assessing your progress in life and course correcting as needed will keep you from getting too out of sync with your intentions. In Chapter Nine I discuss stepping away and doing this important work. You must be willing to create the time and the space for perspective. With each challenging life experience, we are crossing a bridge from one side to the other. In order to learn and grow, take the time to look back and see where you have been and how far you have come. How often do we pat ourselves on the back for our accomplishments? I believe not often enough. Take the time to personally celebrate these milestones, even if it feels silly to you. Our family makes celebrations around the crossings that are difficult as much as the accomplishments. It is in the difficult crossings that we earn our true merit badges and gain wisdom and knowledge. We are then capable of being the field guides to others, having navigated the treacherous waters on our own.

All of this work is about transformation.

GRATITUDE AND APPRECIATION

We are incredibly grateful when good fortune comes our way. Miracles occur every day on this planet and blessings abound. It's so easy to be grateful when things are going swimmingly. However, when we encounter the dark night of the soul, or our misfortunes seem to be piling up all at once, the magic and blessings seem to disappear. The truth is that each of our experiences, good or bad, has a silver lining in terms of what we learn. Usually, we grow the most from the most difficult circumstances including heartbreak, loss, grief, illness, and our own mistakes.

Our pain is the catalyst for our compassion when we allow it to flow through us. The loss we endure opens our hearts wide to the pain of others. We are better, more loving, empathetic beings on the other side of that pain. When we lose our jobs or our fortunes, we really understand what is important. It is our strength, character, resilience and fortitude that give us the ability to rebuild ourselves. None of these experiences are easy, but they give us grace and understanding of human suffering.

Counting our blessings whether they are exactly what we asked for or not what we bargained for, is an extremely powerful and transformational practice. I can always find at least five things to be grateful for each day despite how poorly my day goes. Be grateful for everything that you have in your life, for the collective experiences that are woven in your tapestry, and for the miracles yet to come. I believe our own health and well-being and our relationships are the greatest assets that we can acquire in our lives. Everything else is just the icing on the cake. Keep a daily gratitude journal and you will feel increasingly blessed day by day.

FINAL THOUGHTS ON LASTING CHANGE

Lasting changes come from knowing ourselves well, honoring our own authenticity, and prioritizing our needs to live fully with self-care and love. Without understanding where we are in relation to where we want to be, we lack the inspired momentum to find peace, calm and wellness in our lives. The responsibility for your peace and well-being is within you. Do not turn this awesome power over to anyone or anything outside of yourself.

Be gentle with yourself as you explore and implement these practices in your life. You have been through a lot, dear soul. This season of your life may seem too demanding and you may find all of this to be too much, but that is not the intention. Thoughtfully choose small changes that work for you to cultivate self-compassion, nurturing, and wellness. Choose quality over quantity for enduring change. Little actions add up over time and you will transform the quality of your life through consistency. The pain will pass you by and grace, resilience and fortitude will take its place. You are an extraordinary being with a mission here on earth. Despite what you think, you are doing a great job. We need your magnificence and light at this time.

Honor that sacred part of yourself that yearns to retreat to the oasis and drink from the source of well-being.

FINAL FIELD NOTES

*"Only when normal things are not normal anymore do
we realize how special things are."*
—UNKNOWN

As I write these words, the pandemic is still not under
control in the United States or much of the world for
that matter. Businesses are collapsing under the strain
of lockdowns and restrictions. The economic forecast
remains unclear, at best. These collective experiences
bring us anxiety, stress, and leave us wondering whether
our future will be brighter or dimmer than our past. Most
of us have never experienced anything like this before.
Our kids are going to school remotely, hopefully not
falling behind. Our ability to get together and celebrate,
praise or mourn has been drastically inhibited. People
feel isolated, depressed and in despair. These events are

very real and entirely out of our control. That does not even account for what we are experiencing individually. Each of us have our own set of challenges, adversities, and circumstances to address.

We may not like what has been served up in this season of our lives. We do not know how this story ends. Whether we are experiencing uncertainty, stress, or a host of other emotions, it is up to each of us to protect ourselves and prepare for our individual, as well as our collective, journey through this challenging time. We can manage our stress and our well-being because that *is* within our control.

Retreating is a gift that you give yourself as well as others. To nurture and support your needs means you can be your best self and share your light with others. By implementing even one of the seven practices in this book, we are that much closer to filling our wellspring. If we can take a step back (or away) and experiment with even a few of these practices, we can confidently restore ourselves in our times of need.

Know that you are never alone in your journey even when you feel desperate loneliness. There is an incredible rooted heart community that exists beyond you, souls that have walked in your shoes and know your pain and despair. There are incredible resources available and accessible to you the moment you acknowledge your need for support, guidance and inspiration. I too have walked in your shoes and have found support from teachers, friends, strangers and by the grace of God. My heart's mission is to help you through your journey.

In spite of the uncertainty of the present moment, I am incredibly optimistic. Foundational changes are underway to reform outdated institutions and mindsets. This is a time for vision and seeing things for what they really are. In the stripping away of outgrown norms we will find lasting, sustainable living on this planet and better ways to serve humanity. I believe that what will arise for each of us will be better and more beautiful than what we have known before. Our collective experiences will teach us to be more compassionate.

You are an important part of this time and have an important role to play so take impeccable care of yourself. Drink from the well. Nourish your mind, your body, and your spirit. Reflect on where you are, where you have been, and where you are going. Course correct as needed. Slow down and rest, cultivate awareness and breathe. Find awe in every day. Wander often and wonder always. Step away for a moment, a day, a week, or longer. Go with the flow and tune up your body on a regular basis. Let energy move through you. Enrich yourself in ways that soothe your heart. Explore as much as you can while you are here on this planet. Connect with and embrace the community around you. Root your heart deep into the earth by inspiring and serving others.

I wish you well on this collective journey and hope to see you along the way.

BIBLIOGRAPHY / REFERENCES

CHAPTER TWO:

- *The Art of Peace: Teachings of the Founder of Aikido*
  1992,English M. Ueshiba, J. Stevens
- *Training the Samurai Mind: A Bushido Sourcebook*
  2009, English, T. Cleary
- *The Book of Five Rings*
  2012,English, M. Musashi, S. Tsujimura, W.S. Wilson

CHAPTER FOUR:

- *Birds Through an Opera Glass*
  2018, English, F.M. Bailey

CHAPTER SIX:

- *Almost Everything: Notes on Hope*
  2018, English, A. Lamott
- *Why We Sleep: Unlocking the Power of Sleep and Dreams*
  2018, English, W.M. PhD

Resources for breathwork:

- https://www.goodtherapy.org/learn-about-therapy/
  types/breathwork#Types%20of%20Breathwork%20
  Approaches%20in%20Therapy
- https://www.healthline.com/health/breathing-
  exercise#pursed-lip-breathing

CHAPTER SEVEN:

- *The Whole30: The 30-Day Guide to Total Health and Food Freedom*
  2015, English, H.M. Urban, D. Hartwig
- *The Case for Keto: Rethinking Weight Control and the Science and Practice of Low-Carb/High-Fat Eating*, 2020, English, G. Taubes
- *The Mozart Effect: Tapping the Power of Music to Heal the Body, Strengthen the Mind, and Unlock the Creative Spirit*, 2001, English, D. Campbell

CHAPTER EIGHT:

- Proceedings of the National Academy of Sciences (PNAS) in 2019:
  reference: https://www.pnas.org/content/116/11/5188
- *100 Parks, 5,000 Ideas: Where to Go, When to Go, What to See, What to Do*
  2019, English, J. Yogerst

CHAPTER NINE:

How to Create a Home Retreat
- https://www.tarabrach.com/create-home-retreat/#sampleschedule)

Online Magazine References:
- Breathe
  https://www.breathemagazine.com
- Organic Spa Magazine
  https://www.organicspamagazine.com

- Yogajournal
  https://www.yogajournal.com
- Online Wellness Retreat Resource
  https://retreat.guru

Meditation Retreats:
- Ananda in the Himalayas - Uttaranchal, India
  https://www.anandaspa.com/en/home
- Green Gulch Farm Zen Center - Muir Beach, CA
  https://www.sfzc.org/practice-centers/green-gulch-farm
- Insight Meditation Society - Barre, Massachusetts
  https://www.dharma.org
- Holy Isle of Arran - Isle of Arran, Scotland
  https://www.holyisle.org
- Miraval - Tucson, Arizona and Austin, Texas
  https://www.miravalresorts.com
- Muktawan 7 Day Meditation Retreat - Phuket, Thailand
  https://meditationforyourself.wordpress.com/2015/04/28/muktawan-retreat/
- Osho Meditation Resort - Pune, India
  https://www.osho.com/osho-meditation-resort
- Rolling Meadows Meditation Retreats - Tulum, Mexico
  https://rollingmeadowsretreat.com
- Simple Peace - Assisi, Italy
  https://www.assisiretreats.org
- Shambhala Mountain Center - Red Feather Lakes, Colorado
  https://www.shambhalamountain.org
- Stillpoint Lodge - Halibut Cove, Alaska
  https://stillpointlodge.com
- The Raj Ayurveda Health Spa - Fairfield, Iowa
  https://theraj.com

- Travaasa - Maui, Hawaii and Austin, Texas
  https://travaasa.com/hana/

Yoga Retreats

- Anamaya Resort - Costa Rica
  https://anamaya.com
- Ananda Spa - India
  https://www.anandaspa.com/en/home
- Bali Spirit Festival - Bali
  https://www.balispiritfestival.com
- Blue Osa - Costa Rica
  https://www.blueosa.com/about-us/
- Civana Wellness Resort and Spa
  https://civanacarefree.com
- Omega Institute - New York
  https://www.eomega.org
- Phool Chatti Ashram, India
  https://www.phoolchattiyoga.com
- Santosha Yoga Retreat - British Columbia
  https://santosha-yoga-retreats.com
- Skylagoon - Iceland
  https://www.skylagoon.com
- Suncokret Retreats - Croatia
  https://www.suncokretdream.net
- The Sanctuary - Thailand
  https://www.thesanctuarythailand.com
- Zuna Yoga Teacher Training - Bali
  https://www.zunayoga.com

Wellness Institutes

- Center for Health and Wellbeing
  https://yourhealthandwellbeing.org

- Chopra Center
  https://chopra.com
- Civana Wellness Resort and Spa
  https://civanacarefree.com
- Esalen Institute - Big Sur, California
  https://www.esalen.org
- Global Wellness Institute
  http://globalwellnessinstitute.org
- Kripalu Center for Yoga and Health
  https://kripalu.org
- Maharishi International University
  https://www.miu.edu
- National Wellness Institute
  https://nationalwellness.org
- Omega Institute
  https://www.eomega.org
- Smith Center for Healing and the Arts
  https://smithcenter.org
- The Well
  https://www.the-well.com
- UCLA Mindful Awareness Research Center (MARC) -
  https://www.uclahealth.org/marc/
- 1440 Multiversity
  https://www.1440.org

List of Integrative Health Centers in every state:

- Resource:
  https://www.researchforwellness.com/health-centers
- Optimum Health Institute
  http://www.optimumhealth.org

Wellness Retreats

- Canyon Ranch Spa
  https://www.canyonranch.com
- Diamond Lodge - Belize
  https://www.diamondlodgebelize.com
- Journey to Sacred Iceland
  https://www.madeleinemarentette.com/journey-to-sacred-iceland-trip
- Le Monaste`re des Augustines, Quebec City
  https://monastere.ca/en
- Pritkin Longevity Center and Spa - Miami, Florida
  https://www.pritikin.com
- Skyterra Wellness Retreat - North Carolina
  https://skyterrawellness.com
- Velas Resorts - Puerto Vallarta, Mexico
  https://www.velasresorts.com/spas

Wellness focused Travel Agencies

- https://www.fountain-of-you.com
- https://www.journeysthatfit.com
- https://lotustrips.com
- https://www.mytripwell.com
- http://souljournadventure.com
- https://www.suitedreamstravel.net
- https://vacayou.com
- https://www.vipwellnessgetaways.com
- https://www.wellnesstourismassociation.org

CHAPTER TEN:

- Cranial Sacral Therapy benefits, Cleveland Clinic
  https://www.my.clevelandclinic.org/heath/
  treatments/17677-cranialsacral-therapy

- Rolfing, pioneer Dr. Ida Rolf, PhD
  http://www/rolf.org/rolfing.php
- Dr. Ida Rolf Institute
  http://www.rolf.org
- Tai Chi benefits, Harvard Medical Center
  https://www.health.Harvard.edu/staying-healthy/the-
  health-benefits-of-tai-chi
- Somatic Healing, Dr. Peter A. Levine, PhD
  https://www.somaticexperiencing.com
- Johns Hopkins Medicine
  https://www.hopkinsmedicine.org/integrative_medicine_
  digestive_center/services/therapeutic_massage.html
- The six branches of yoga
  https://www.medicalnewstoday.com

Tai Chi Resources

- Tai Chi Health:
  https://www.Taichihealth.com

- The Tree of Life Tai Chi Center:
  https://www.treeoflifetaichi.com

- Jake Mace Tai Chi:
  https://www.youtube.com/watch?v=6w7IS8_UzHM&t=23s

Qigong Resources

- Qigong Institute:
  https://www.qigonginstitute.org

- Spring Forest Qigong:
  https://www.springforestqigong.com

CHAPTER ELEVEN:

How to Make a Vision Board

- Christine Kane Blog:
  https://christinekane.com/how-to-make-a-vision-board/#sthash.iNO5AzHG.uiuotyNc.dpbs

Goal and Dream Planning

- Cultivate What Matters Powersheets and planning with Lara Casey: https://cultivatewhatmatters.com
- *Everything is Figureoutable* by Marie Forleo:
  https://www.marieforleo.com/2016/05/everything-is-figureoutable/

CHAPTER TWELVE:

- *The Hidden Life of Trees: What They Feel, How They Communicate - Discoveries from A Secret World* (The Mysteries of Nature, 1), 2016, English, P. Wohlleben, J. Billinghurst, T. Flannery, S. Simard
- National Institute of Health:
  https://www.ncbi.nim.nih.gov
- Substance Abuse and Mental Health Services:
  https://www.SAMHSA.gov
- The Center for Compassion and Altruism Research and Education, Stanford University:
  http://ccare.stanford.edu/video/campus-conversations-on-compassion/
- SAMHSA's National Helpline – 1-800-662-HELP (4357) SAMHSA's National Helpline is a free, confidential, 24/7, 365-day-a-year treatment referral and information service (in English and Spanish) for individuals and families facing mental and/or substance use disorders.

- Addiction Technology Transfer Center (ATTC) offers a session on Addiction Recovery and Intimate Violence https://healtheknowledge.org/course/view.php?id=18

- The National Hispanic and Latino ATTC recorded a webinar this February on the "Intersection of Domestic Violence or Intimate Partner Violence and Addiction" https://attcnetwork.org/centers/national-hispanic-and-latino-attc/product/intersection- domestic-violence-or-intimate

- Substance Abuse Treatment and Domestic Violence - Quick Guide for Clinicians Based on TIP 25 https://store.samhsa.gov/product/Substance-Abuse-Treatment-and- Domestic-Violence/sma15-3583

- The National Center on Domestic Violence, Trauma & Mental Health, a SAMHSA partner, recently released: Supporting Survivors' Access to Substance Use Disorder and Mental Health Services During the COVID-19 Emergency http://www.nationalcenterdvtraumamh.org/2020/03/covid-19-resources-for- advocates/

Other non-SAMHSA Resources:

- Crisis Response Network - Grief and Loss https://www.crisisnetwork.org/find-help/behavioral-health-conditions/grief-and-loss/

- Grief Resource Network https://www.griefresourcenetwork.com/crisis-center/hotlines/

- National Center for State Courts: https://www.ncsc.org/topics/children-families-and-elders/marriage-divorce-and-custody/resource-guide

- National Domestic Violence Hotline Phone number: 1-800-799-SAFE (7233)

- National Family Solutions - Divorce Help and Resources
  https://www.nationalfamilysolutions.com/divorce-help/

- The National Institute on Drug Abuse
  https://www.drugabuse.gov/publications/principles-drug-addiction-treatment-research-based-guide-third-edition/resources

- The National Network to Eliminate Domestic Violence
  https://nnedv.org

- National Prevention Resources
  https://nasadad.org/prevention-resources/

- Department of Justice, Office of Women's Health
  Resources on Domestic Violence

- Prevent Child Abuse America
  Coronavirus Resources & Tips for Parents, Children & Others

- Stronghearts Native Helpline
  1-844-762-8483

- Suicide Prevention Hotlne
  1-800-273-8255

ACKNOWLEDGMENTS

I thank and honor the extraordinary team of individuals who helped me breathe life into this book. My editor Judie Stillman guided me through multiple enhancements and curated edits that allow the message and vision of the book to shine. Little did I know that our collaboration would be so enriched and supported by our personal journeys with our own parents this past year.

To Rachel Grant, my gifted and talented artist and illustrator across the pond who has soulfully captured the essence of the feelings I wanted to convey with this guide. I found Rachel's artwork by happenstance and realized through our collaboration that we are living by the same guiding principles of life. Nothing is by accident.

To Tracy Moran, my soul sister in spirit, who gave me profound inspiration for this season of life and the articulation and expression of my unique gifts. Without your support and encouragement, I would still be trying to figure out who I want to be when I grow up.

To Sarah Beaudin, for your assistance and support in getting me to the finish line so that this manuscript actually became a published book. Thank you for your ongoing guidance and mentoring in the "final chapter".

To Chad Poggioli, for the beautiful design and branding for The Art of Retreating website which simultaneously captures the feeling of simplicity and adventure. Thank you for articulating what was in my imagination.

To my ground support team and trailblazers: Kristan Fazio for your spirit and enthusiasm to explore with me what's around the next corner; Leena Patidar for your rooted heart and for connecting me with Judie Stillman; Chris Morris, for your healing alchemy for my mind, body and spirit. You put all the pieces of me back together so that I can bring my warrior spirit back into the ring of life; Margaret Pope, for inspiring me with your own journey of healing; To my rooted heart community of friends and family who enrich my days spent well on this Earth.

To my mother Lee Smith who gave me nurturing love, a spirit of hospitality and celebration, and the gift of the written word; To my father Peter Smith who embodies unconditional love, zest for life, and grace. You are still teaching all of us life's lessons. To my siblings Michael, Kathleen and Peter for your love and support throughout our lives. I honor the sacredness of each of our unique souls and perspective on life.

My husband and best friend, Mark. Without you by my side, I would be lost in the wilderness. Thank you for supporting all of my dreams, traveling by my side and trying out all of my wild hair ideas and explorations! Our children are blessed to call you dad.

And finally, my children Emily and Jake, my greatest teachers about myself and the reasons why I want to make the world a better place.

ABOUT THE AUTHOR

Jacqueline Heil is an artist and writer living in southern California. Time is spent creating and planning experiences, traveling and exploring and researching ways to cultivate an enriching life. She has broad experience with event planning including conducting retreats, conferences and organizational planning. Her early career began in high tech corporate finance after attending Fairfield University where she received a degree in financial management. She also attended the Design Institute of San Diego. Later she worked in executive operations for a nonprofit organization with children facing adversity, and observed the positive impact of art and music enrichment as healing aspects of childrens' lives. During that time, she was part of the 2012 Oscar award winning short documentary film INOCENTE. She has spent the last few years as an operations director of a global meditation institute.

Jacqueline lives on a ranch with her husband Mark and her dog Harley and a menagerie of other animals. She and her husband are creating a sanctuary and community for both restfulness and enriching activities that bring joy to others' lives.

ABOUT THE ARTIST

Rachel Grant is a mixed media artist based in North Staffordshire UK. She is inspired by slow, simple, seasonal living and aims to capture moments of calm in everything she creates.

www.rachel-grant.com

CONTINUE YOUR JOURNEY

For ever changing resources, inspiration and support,
visit the Art of Retreating website at:

https://www.artofretreating.com

WHAT DID YOU THINK OF
THE ART OF RETREATING?

I am extremely grateful you selected this book to read knowing that your time is of value and you have the opportunity to choose from any number of books. I hope it added value and provided resources for your journey.

If you enjoyed this book and found some benefit in reading it, I'd love to hear from you through the website or one of our social media platforms.

🔗 https://www.artofretreating.com

📷 artofretreating

ⓕ Jacquie Smith Heil

Please share this book with friends and family as well as take some time to post a review on Amazon or Goodreads which boosts the visibility of the book on these platforms.

With Gratitude,

Jacquie Heil

Made in the USA
Las Vegas, NV
14 November 2021